★★★ SixTH Edition ★★★

THE LAW

[in Plain English]®

for

Crafts

Leonard D. DuBoff

[attorney-at-law]

ALLWORTH PRESS
NEW YORK

DEDICATION

*This book is dedicated to some of the most important people in my world:
to my mother and father, Millicent and Rubin, for the gift of life;
to my wife, Mary Ann, for her caring, support, inspiration and assistance;
to my children, Colleen Rose, Robert Courtney, and Sabrina Ashley,
for their love, friendship and inspiration; and to my grandchildren,
Brian Michael and Taliek Isaiah, so that they can carry on the tradition.*

09 08 07 06 05   5 4 3 2 1

Published by Allworth Press
An imprint of Allworth Communications
10 East 23rd Street, New York, NY 10010

Cover design by Derek Bacchus
Page composition/typography by SR Desktop Services, Ridge, NY

ISBN: 1-58115-424-0

Library of Congress Catalog-in-Publication Data
DuBoff, Leonard D.
     The law (in plain English) for crafts / Leonard D. Duboff.—6th ed.
          p.   cm.
     Includes index.
     1. Artisans—Legal status, laws, etc.—United States.   2. Law—United States.
     3. Handicraft—Law and legislation—United States.   I. Title.

     KF390.A69D8   2005
     349.73'02'4745—dc22

                                                    2005014096

Printed in Canada

CONTENTS

FOREWORD

Too often, our failure to succeed as crafts professionals lies not in
the absence of talent or skills, but in resistance to acquiring a
knowledge of sound business practices—especially those related
to law and contracts. Like it or not, artists and artisans are as involved
as other professionals in business and business law. Because art is at best
a precarious means of life support, we require familiarity with applicable
law in order to proceed easily and confidently in business transactions.

As artists, we have a perennial tendency to spurn all conventional
wisdom, to treat business dealings with the same spirit of adventure with
which we develop media or style. Reinventing the wheel of business
practice does not work as well as we would like, and being unclear in
contractual matters makes us all the more vulnerable in transactions in
which we commit our resources and our futures.

We confuse probing experimentally *with* a medium with methods of
negotiating *outside* it—that is, with *others*. Within media, we make, in a
brief period, many trials and many errors. We learn from the direct
cause-and-effect process typical of crafts, and we move on. Because business transactions involve additional elements (notably other people,
their practices, *their* memory, and mores), we must learn how to deal
directly and successfully with them.

Because I learned too slowly the implications of business law and am
only recently as at ease with contracts as with crafts, I am pleased about
this book. Now, all of us can learn from others' experiences—interpreted
specifically for our special audience. Here it is; a viable tool in itself and
invaluable to the Standards of Practice that the American Craft Council
is (at last) developing.

Jack Lenor Larsen
President/American Craft Council

PREFACE

More than a quarter of a century ago, the bonding of two apparently dissimilar fields, art and law, began. While it is impossible to identify the precise point when this union occurred, it is easy to spot several events that were significant in bringing about the merger. For some curious reason, the factors that contributed to what is today the discipline of art law were spontaneous, covered a broad geographic area and, in some cases, occurred simultaneously. For example, in 1969 three New York lawyers perceived that creative people needed a special kind of legal representation that was not then available. These attorneys formed the first Volunteer Lawyers for the Arts (VLA), and the concept quickly spread throughout the United States and Europe.

The evolutionary process that resulted in the art law discipline involved educators as well as lawyers. Students in many colleges and universities are now being offered an opportunity to take courses in this field on both undergraduate and graduate levels.

In the mid-seventies, the Association of American Law Schools created an art law section, thus providing law professors with a forum within which to exchange ideas about the field. Many of their proceedings have been published in scholarly journals, and some have become part of the Congressional Record. Today, many law students are being trained as art lawyers.

The increase in activity in this area has resulted in special legislation. Laws on art, at both the federal and state levels, are appearing at an increasing rate. Periodicals and professional journals for artists and craftsworkers regularly carry articles on the law as it affects them, and these articles have been very well received. Although many books on art law are now available, very little has been published that is up-to-date and specifically aimed at the needs and interests of professional craftspeople.

Today, more than ever, these needs are compelling. Crafts have become extremely popular, and the industry is expanding. With trade shows specifically dedicated to crafts and traditional gift shows containing crafts sections, the number of individuals involved in the industry has increased. There is also a need for education in this expanded field. Seminars on crafts law help fill this need, but they are sporadic. This book is intended to be a ready reference for professionals in the crafts business who desire an explanation "in plain English" of the numerous legal issues they encounter in their day-to-day business activities.

This project began in 1984, when the late Michael Scott, a pioneer in the crafts industry, urged me to write this book in order to fill the void he perceived in this area. It has been periodically updated, and today it is hoped that this sixth edition of The Law (in Plain English)® for Crafts will continue the tradition of providing you, the reader, with a useful and understandable tool. In addition to updating and expanding the text of this work, I have combined it with Business and Legal Forms (in Plain English)® for Craftspeople to provide you with a single volume that contains both explanatory material and practical forms.

The task of compiling the source material and working on the revisions of this volume included numerous individuals' efforts. While it is impossible to identify them all, some deserve special recognition. I would like to extend my special thanks to Christy O. King, Esq., of The DuBoff Law Group, who assisted with verification of many technical aspects of this revision. I would also like to thank Lynn Della for her yeoman's task in working with me on a regular basis in hammering out this revision; the project could not have been completed without her. Peggy M. Reckow of The DuBoff Law Group was extremely helpful in formatting this work.

I was fortunate to have the aid of other professionals when working on this revision. These experts added a great deal to the quality of this work and deserve kudos for their efforts. They include: Mary Culshaw of the accounting firm of Napier & Associates; John Stevko, CPA of the consulting firm of Stevko & Associates; Michael H. DuBoff, Esq., of the law firm of Snow Becker Krauss, PC; and Donald Davies, Director of Technology for The DuBoff Law Group, for his technical assistance. As this manuscript was going to press, the President signed a new bankruptcy law which made significant changes in the field of bankruptcy. I was, therefore, fortunate to have the aid of Thomas M. Renn, Esq., an attorney and bankruptcy trustee who has authored a prominent book on bankruptcy law and is a prestigious member of the Bankruptcy Bar, assist me in understanding the new code and revising the galleys to reflect the changes.

Finally, I would like to thank my partner in law and life, Mary Ann Crawford DuBoff, for all that she has done to help with this project. It could never have been completed without her.

1
FORMS OF ORGANIZATION

Many craftsworkers are particularly happy in their profession because they believe they have escaped the stultifying atmosphere of the gray-suit business world. But they have not escaped it entirely. The same laws that govern the billion-dollar auto industry govern the craftsperson. In this chapter on organizing a business, I will discuss ways of using business law to your advantage.

All craftsworkers know that to survive in business, they must carefully plan their money matters, yet few craftsmakers realize the importance of planning the *form* of the business enterprise itself. Most craftspeople have little need of the sophisticated organizational structure used in industry, but since craftspeople must pay taxes, take out loans, and expose themselves to uncertain liabilities with every sale they make, it only makes sense to structure the business in such a way as to minimize these worries.

Every business has an organizational form best suited to it. When I counsel craftspeople on organizing their businesses, I usually go about it in two steps. First, we discuss various aspects of tax and liability in order to decide which of the basic forms is best. There are only a handful of basic forms: the *sole proprietorship*, the *partnership*, the *corporation*, the *limited liability company*, the *limited liability partnership*, and a few hybrids. Once we decide which of these is most appropriate, we can go into the organizational details—like partnership agreements or corporate bylaws. These define the day-to-day operations of the business and, therefore, must be tailored to individual situations.

What I will do here is explain some of the basic features of typical business organizations with respect to their advantages and disadvantages. Much of what follows will anticipate problems, but, since full discussion of the more intricate details cannot be given here, a craftsmaker should consult an experienced business attorney before attempting to adopt any particular structure. My main purpose is to assist you in communicating your wishes to your lawyer and to enable you to understand the options available.

THE AMERICAN DREAM: SOLE PROPRIETORSHIP

The technical name for this form of business may be unfamiliar to you, but chances are it is the form under which you operate now. The sole proprietorship is an unincorporated business owned by one person. Though not peculiar to the United States, it was, and still is, the essence of the American dream—for personal freedom follows economic freedom. As a form of business, it is elegant in its simplicity. Legal requirements are few and simple. In most localities, in order to operate a business, you must obtain a license from the city or county, which usually entails no more than paying a small fee. If you wish to operate the business under a name other than your own, the name must be registered with the state and/or the county in which you are doing business. With these details taken care of, you are legally in business.

Disadvantages of Sole Proprietorship

There are numerous pitfalls involved in operating your business as a sole proprietorship. If these dangers are sufficiently real in your case, you probably should consider the other forms of organization discussed later in this chapter.

If you are the sole proprietor of a venture, your personal property is at stake. If for any reason you owe more than the dollar value of your business, your creditors may be able to take most of your personal property to satisfy the debts. In many cases, insurance can be obtained that will shift the loss from you to the insurance company, but there are some risks for which no insurance can be obtained. For instance, no insurance can be purchased to protect against a large rise in costs or sudden unavailability of supplies or raw materials. Insurance premiums can be quite high, and it is impossible to predict premium increases. These, as well as many other factors, can drive a business, and thus the sole proprietor, into bankruptcy.

Taxes

Before leaving the area of the sole proprietorship, I must briefly deal with taxes. The sole proprietor is taxed on all business profits and may deduct losses. The rate of tax paid will increase as income increases. Fortunately, there are some methods to lessen this tax burden, such as establishing an approved pension plan.

THE PARTNERSHIP

A partnership is defined by most state laws as an association of two or more persons to conduct, as co-owners, a business for profit. It can be an attractive arrangement, because partners pool money, supplies, and professional contacts. No formalities are required. In fact, there are cases where people have been held to be partners even though they had no intention of forming a partnership. For example, if you lend a friend some money to start a business and the friend agrees to pay you a certain percentage of whatever profit is made, you may be your friend's partner in the eyes of the law, even though you take no further interest in the business. This is important, because each partner is subject to unlimited personal liability for the debts of the partnership. Also, each partner is liable for the negligence of another partner and of the partnership's employees when the negligent act occurred in the usual course of business.

From this, two things should be obvious. First, since the addition of a partner increases your potential liability, significant care should be exercised in finding a responsible partner. Second, the partnership should be adequately insured to protect both the assets of the partnership and the personal assets of each partner. It is a good idea to draw up a written partnership agreement to avoid future confusion or misunderstandings.

As mentioned above, no formalities are required to create a partnership. Where there is no formal agreement defining the terms of the partnership, such as control of the partnership or the distribution of profits, state law supplies the terms. State laws are based on the fundamental characteristics of the typical partnership throughout the ages and are, therefore, thought to correspond to the reasonable expectations of the partners. The most important of these presumed characteristics are:

- No one can become a member of a partnership without the unanimous consent of all partners.
- All members have an equal vote in the management of the partnership regardless of the size of their interest in it.
- All partners share equally in the profits and losses of the partnership, no matter how much capital they contribute.
- A simple majority vote is required for decisions in the ordinary course of business, and a unanimous vote is required to change the fundamental character of the business.

• A partnership is terminable at will by any partner. If a partner with-draws, the partnership is legally dissolved.

Most state laws contain a provision that allows the partners to make their own agreement in order to work out the management structure and division of profits which best suit the needs of their individual partnership.

The Eight Basics of a Partnership Agreement

1. The Name of the Partnership

Most partnerships simply use the surnames of the major partners. The choice here is nothing more than the order of names. Various factors can be considered, from prestige to euphony. If a name other than the part-ners' is used, then it will be necessary to file that assumed business name with the state and/or county. (An assumed business name is sometimes known as a fictitious business name, and is often referred to as "DBA" or "d/b/a," meaning "doing business as.") Care should be taken to choose a name that is distinctive and not already in use. If the name is not suffi-ciently distinctive, others can use confusingly similar names; if the name is already in use, you may become liable for trade-name infringement.

2. A Description of the Business

The partners should agree on the basic scope of the business—its requirements with regard to capital and labor, the parties' individual contributions of capital and labor, and perhaps some plans regarding future growth.

3. Partnership Capital

After determining how much capital is to be contributed, the partners must decide when it will be contributed, how to value the property con-tributed, and whether there is to be a right to contribute more or to withdraw any at a later date.

4. Duration of the Partnership

Partnerships may be organized for a fixed duration or automatically dis-solved upon certain conditions.

5. Distribution of Profits

Any scheme for distribution of profits can be arranged. Although ordi-narily a partner does not receive a salary, it is possible to give an active partner a guaranteed salary in addition to a share of the profits. Since the partnership's profits can be determined only at the close of a business year, ordinarily, no distribution is made until that time. However, the partners may be given a monthly draw of money against their final share of profits. In some cases, it may be appropriate to allow limited expense accounts for partners.

Not all of the profits of the partnership need be distributed at year's end. Some can be retained for expansion. This can be provided for in the partnership agreement. It should be noted that regardless of whether the profits are distributed or not, each partner must pay tax on his or her designated share. The IRS refers directly to the partnership agreement to determine what constitutes each partner's share—this shows how important a partnership agreement is.

6. Management

The division of power in the partnership can be made in many ways. All partners can be given an equal voice, or some may have more authority than others. A few partners may be allowed to manage the business entirely, with the remaining partners being given a vote only on predesignated issues. Besides voting, three other areas of management should be covered. First is the question of who can sign checks, place orders, or sell partnership property. Under state partnership laws, any partner may do these things, as long as they are done in the usual course of business, but such a broad delegation of authority can lead to confusion, so it may be best to delegate this authority more narrowly.

Second, it is a good idea to determine a regular date for partnership meetings. Third, some consideration should be given to the possibility of a dispute among the partners leading to a deadlocked vote. One way to avoid this is to distribute the voting power in such a way as to make a deadlock impossible. That would mean, for instance, in a two-person partnership, one partner would be in absolute control, which might be unacceptable to the other partner. If, instead, the power is divided evenly among an even number of partners, as is often the case, the agreement should stipulate a neutral party or arbitrator who can settle the dispute and, thereby, often avoid a dissolution of the partnership.

7. Prohibited Acts

A list of prohibited acts, elaborating and expanding on three fundamental duties that each partner owes the partnership by virtue of being an agent of the partnership, should be made a part of the partnership agreement.

The first duty is that of diligence. This means the partner must exercise reasonable care in acting as a partner.

Second is the duty of obedience. The partner must obey the rules that the partnership has promulgated and, more importantly, must not exceed the authority that the partnership has vested in her or him.

Finally, there is a duty of loyalty. A partner may not, without approval of the other partners, compete with the partnership in another business. He or she may not seize upon a business opportunity that would be of value to the partnership without first disclosing the opportunity to the partnership and allowing the partnership to pursue it, if the partnership so desires.

8. Dissolution and Liquidation

A partnership is automatically dissolved upon the death, withdrawal, expulsion, or request of a partner. Dissolution identifies the legal end of the partnership, but need not affect its economic life if the partners provide for the continuation of the business after a dissolution. Nonetheless, a dissolution will affect the business, because the partner who withdraws or is expelled, or the estate of a deceased partner, will be entitled to a return of that partner's share of the total capital of the partnership. How this capital is to be returned should be decided before the dissolution, for it may be impossible to negotiate afterward.

One method of handling this is to provide for a return of capital in cash over a period of time. After a partner leaves, the partnership may need to be reorganized and recapitalized. Some provision should be made to define in what proportion the remaining partners may purchase the interest of the departed partner. Finally, since it is always possible that the partners will desire to liquidate the partnership, it should be decided in advance who will liquidate the assets, what assets will be distributed as such, and what property will be returned to its original contributor.

As you can see, a comprehensive partnership agreement is no simple matter. It is, in fact, essential for potential partners to devote some time to preparation of an agreement and to enlist the services of a competent business lawyer. For the initial expense of a lawyer who puts together an agreement suited to the needs of your partnership, you will save many times the legal fees through the smooth organization, operation, and final dissolution of your partnership.

Advantages and Disadvantages of Partnership

The economic advantages of doing business in a partnership are the pooling of capital, greater ease in obtaining credit because of the collective credit rating, and a potentially more efficient allocation of labor and resources. A major disadvantage is that each partner is fully and personally liable for all the debts of the partnership—even if he or she was not personally involved in incurring those debts.

A partnership does not possess any special tax advantages over a sole proprietorship. As a partner, you will pay a personal income tax on your share of the profits whether they are distributed or not. In turn, each partner is entitled to the same proportion of the partnership deductions and credits. The partnership must prepare an annual information tax return known as Schedule Kl, Form 1065, which details each partner's share of income, credits, and deductions and against which the IRS can check the individual returns filed by the partners.

Limited Liability Partnerships

For businesses that have been conducted in the partnership form and also desire a liability shield, the limited liability partnership, or LLP, is now available. This business form parallels the limited liability company (LLC, see page 14) in most respects, although it is created by converting a partnership into an LLP and is frequently available for professionals who, in many states, may not conduct business through LLCs.

Licensed professionals who desire some form of liability shield may also create professional corporations. These business entities do not generally have the same liability shields available to business corporations. When LLCs were first created, most professional associations declared them analogous to business corporations and thus prohibited their use by professionals, though a few states now allow professional LLCs. The LLP, on the other hand, has been created as a business form permitted for all professionals.

THE LIMITED PARTNERSHIP

The limited partnership is a hybrid structure containing elements of both the partnership and corporation. A limited partnership may be formed by parties who wish to invest in a partnership and, in return, to share in its profits, but who seek to limit their risk to the amount of their investment. The law provides for such limited risk, but only so long as the limited partner plays no active role in the day-to-day management and operation of the business. In effect, the limited partner is very much like an investor who buys a few shares of stock in a corporation but has no significant role in running the company. For a limited partnership to exist, it is necessary to have one or more general partners who run the business and who have full personal liability, as well as one or more limited partners who play a passive role.

In order to form a limited partnership, a certificate must be filed with the appropriate state agency. If the certificate is not filed or is improperly filed, the limited partner could be treated as a general partner and thus lose the protection of limited liability. In addition, the limited partner *must* refrain from trying to influence the policy-making activities of the partnership. Otherwise, the limited partner might be found to be actively participating in the business and, thereby, held to be a general partner with unlimited personal liability.

A limited partnership is a convenient form for securing needed financial backers who wish to share in the profits of an enterprise without undue exposure to personal liability, and when a corporation or limited liability company may not be appropriate, e.g., when one does not meet all the requirements of an S corporation (see page 13) or when one does not desire ownership in an LLC. A limited partnership can be used to attract investors when credit is hard to obtain or is too expensive. In return for investing, the limited partner receives a designated share of the profits. If there are no profits, the limited partner receives nothing, whereas a creditor of the partnership can sue if the partners fail to repay.

Another use of the limited partnership is to facilitate reorganization of a general partnership after the death or retirement of a general partner. Remember, a partnership is terminated upon the death, withdrawal, expulsion, or by the request of any partner. Although the original partnership is thus technically dissolved when one partner retires, it is not uncommon for the remaining partners to agree to buy out the retiring partner's share—that is, to return that person's capital contribution and keep the business going. Raising enough cash to buy out the retiring partner, however, could jeopardize the business by forcing the remaining partners to liquidate certain partnership assets. A convenient way to avoid such a detrimental liquidation is for the retiree to step into limited-partner status. Thus, he or she can continue to share in the profits that, to some extent, flow from that partner's past labor, while removing that partner's personal assets from the risk of partnership liabilities. In the meantime, the remaining partners are afforded the opportunity to restructure the partnership's funding under more favorable conditions.

WHAT YOU DON'T WANT: UNINTENDED PARTNERS

Whether yours is a straightforward partnership or a limited partnership, one arrangement you want to avoid is the unintended partnership. Following are some examples of why an ounce of prevention, in the form of a moderate legal fee, can sometimes save pounds of money and headaches later.

In 1978, Irene Stein, a well-known Colorado artist, went to Moses Sanchez, a retired welder-turned-metal sculptor, and showed him a sketch she allegedly had made. The sketch, which bore a remarkable resemblance to Rosak's *Cradle Song, Variation No. Two* (cataloged in the collection of the Museum of Modern Art), was used by Sanchez only for inspiration. The sculpture he ultimately created bore very little resemblance to the original sketch.

Sanchez was outraged some time later when he was shown a newspaper article with a picture of Mrs. Stein wearing a welder's mask, holding a torch and standing in front of his creation, which the article ascribed to her.

Sanchez sued, alleging that he was the artist. Stein defended on the ground that she was the creator and Sanchez was merely a foundryman who embodied her ideas in a tangible metal form. The contrived shot of Mrs. Stein in the newspaper was never fully explained, though Mrs. Stein suggested that it was the newspaper photographer's idea rather than her own.

The issue presented by this case is by no means a novel one. When, for example, a person commissions a portrait and periodically reviews the artist's progress, recommending additions or changes, can the patron be considered the artist, or at least a collaborator? On the other hand, when the sculptor creates a master image or maquette that is made into a mold and cast by a metal foundry, has the foundryman become a co-creator of the work? Similar examples abound in the crafts world— between the stained-glass designer and the craftsperson who executes the design; or between the weaver of a commissioned wall hanging and the interior decorator who specifies its size, theme, color scheme, and design.

In an early French case, *Guino c. consorts, Renoir*, Guino, an apprentice in Renoir's studio, claimed co-authorship of sculptures he had executed under Renoir's direction. The French court concluded that Guino's own personality was sufficiently imprinted on the works so that they could no longer be considered solely Renoir's creations. Unfortunately, the court did not state how much personality Guino had to imprint to entitle him to claim the right of co-authorship.

Newsweek magazine reported that, toward the end of her life, Georgia O'Keefe's sight was failing and that she merely signed canvases that had been painted by another artist. A New Mexico handyman, John Poling, claimed he had painted three O'Keefe canvases under her instruction.

O'Keefe admitted that Poling physically made the work, but she claimed that he was merely the equivalent of her palette knife.

Another interesting situation arose several years ago when it was admitted that many portraits signed by Charles J. Fox, including those of John F. Kennedy, Justice Brandeis, and other notables, were actually painted by Irving Resnikoff. Fox admitted paying Resnikoff $250 to $300 for each portrait, which he then sold for up to $7,000 apiece. These admissions were made in tax court, where Fox claimed that his profits from the resales were capital gains rather than ordinary income, as the earnings of an artist creating and selling a painting would normally be classified. Fox also attempted to take a business deduction for the amount paid to Resnikoff, the original artist.

Since Fox probably met with the patron or obtained a photograph, conceptualized the project, and merely had Resnikoff execute the final product, should Fox be considered the artist or at least a co-author? The dilemma presented when the person who actually executes the work is different from the one who has the original idea is a difficult one.

In *Sanchez v. Stein*, the issue was resolved by the parties themselves prior to the trial. Mrs. Stein admitted that she was not the creator of the now-famous metal sculpture of a crescent within which three nested eagles reach skyward, which Moses Sanchez, the actual creator, entitled "Winged Wolves." Stein agreed to pay Sanchez a cash settlement and return several other of his works she had in her possession. It would appear that, in this case at least, the person who created the work was acknowledged as the artist.

In *Community for Creative Non-Violence (CCNV) v. Reid*, the Supreme Court held that the individual who executes the work is considered the artist for copyright purposes, although the parties may have agreed before the work began that their individual contributions should result in a joint work (discussed more fully in chapter 10).

Thus, the surest way to avoid unintended partners is to spell out, in a detailed writing, the essentials and expectations of any arrangement into which you enter with another person.

THE CORPORATION

The corporation may sound like a form of business that pertains only to large companies with many employees—an impersonal monster wholly alien to the world of the craftsperson. Whether or not this image corresponds to reality, in essence, there is nothing in the nature of the corporation that requires it. There are advantages and disadvantages to incorporating. If it appears advantageous to incorporate, it can be done with surprising ease and with little expense. Nonetheless, it is necessary to use a lawyer's assistance to ensure that the formalities required by the state are fulfilled, and to be advised on corporate mechanics and payment of the corporation's taxes.

Differences Between a Corporation and a Partnership

In order to discuss the corporation, it is useful to contrast its characteristics with those of a partnership. Perhaps the most important difference is that, like limited partners, the owners of the corporation, or shareholders as they are officially called, are not personally liable for the corporation's debts; they stand to lose only their investments. Unlike a limited partner, a shareholder is allowed full participation in the control of the corporation through the shareholders' voting privileges; the higher the percentage of outstanding shares owned, the more significant the control. This limited liability may be partially illusory for the small corporation, however, because very often creditors will demand that the owners personally co-sign for any credit extended.

While individuals are personally liable for their wrongful acts, even if they are conducting business in the corporate form, they may escape liability if the other party has agreed to hold only the corporation responsible. This corporate liability shield also extends to the wrongful acts of corporate employees. For example, if an assistant negligently injures another person while driving to the clay supplier, the assistant will be liable for the negligent act, and the corporation may be liable as well. The craftsperson who owns the corporation, however, will probably not be personally liable.

The second area of difference is in continuity of existence. The many events that can cause the dissolution of a partnership do not have the same result when they occur within the corporate context. It is common to create a corporation with perpetual existence. Unlike partners, shareholders cannot decide to withdraw and demand a return of their capital from the corporation. Their recourse is to sell their stock, which has no direct impact on the capital of the corporation itself. Therefore, a corporation may have both legal and economic continuity. This can also be a tremendous disadvantage to shareholders or their heirs when a sale of stock is desired and there is no market for the stock. There are, however, agreements that may be used to guarantee a return of capital should a shareholder die or wish to withdraw.

The third difference is the free transferability of ownership. In a partnership, no one can become a partner without the unanimous consent of the other partner(s), unless otherwise agreed in the partnership agreement. In a corporation, however, shareholders can generally sell their shares to whomever they wish. If a small corporation does not want to be open to outside ownership, transferability may be restricted.

The fourth difference is in the structure of management and control. Owners of "common" stock have a vote in proportion to their ownership in the corporation. There are also other kinds of stock that can be created that may or may not have voting rights. A voting shareholder uses his or her vote to elect a board of directors and to create rules under which the board may operate.

The basic rules of the corporation are stated in the articles of incorporation, which are filed with the state. These serve as the constitution for the corporation and can be amended by shareholder vote. More detailed operational rules, called bylaws, should also be prepared. Both shareholders and directors may have power to create or amend bylaws. This varies from state to state. The board of directors then makes operational decisions for the corporation and will probably delegate day-to-day control to a president.

A shareholder, even if he or she owns all the stock in a corporation, may not directly preempt the decision of the board of directors, though in a few more progressive states, a small corporation may entirely forego having a board of directors. In such cases, the corporation is authorized to allow the shareholders to vote on business decisions, just as in a partnership.

At first glance, it may appear that these formalities are not necessary for a small corporation, especially one owned by a single shareholder. Unfortunately, if the corporate formalities are not strictly followed, the corporation's limited liability shield may be lost.

The fifth distinction between a partnership and a corporation is the greater variety of means available to the corporation for raising additional capital. Partnerships are quite restricted in this regard. They can borrow money or, if all partners agree, they can take on additional partners. A corporation, on the other hand, may issue more stock, and this stock can be of many different varieties: recallable at a set price, for example, or convertible into another kind of stock.

A means frequently used to attract a new investor is to issue preferred stock; that is, the corporation agrees to pay the preferred shareholder a predetermined amount before it pays any dividends to other shareholders. Also, if the corporation should go bankrupt, a preferred shareholder will be paid out of the proceeds of liquidation before common shareholders, although after the corporation's employees and general creditors are paid.

The issuance of new stock merely requires, in most cases, approval by a majority of the existing shareholders. In addition, corporations can borrow money on a short-term basis by issuing notes, or for a longer period by issuing debentures or bonds. In fact, a corporation's ability to raise additional capital is limited only by its lawyer's creativity and the economic reality of the marketplace.

The last distinction is the manner in which a corporation is taxed. Under both state and federal laws, the profits of the corporation are taxed to the corporation before they are paid out as dividends. The dividends constitute personal income to the shareholders and are taxed again as such. This double taxation constitutes the major disadvantage of incorporating.

Avoiding Double Taxation

There are several methods to avoid double taxation. First, a corporation can plan its business so as not to show very much profit. This can be done by making payments to shareholders in other capacities. For example, a shareholder can be paid a salary for his or her services, rent for property leased to the corporation, or interest on a loan made to the corporation. All of these are legal deductions from corporate income.

The corporation can also reinvest its profits for reasonable business expansion. This undistributed money is not taxed as income to the shareholders, although the corporation must pay corporate tax on it. By contrast, the retained earnings of a partnership are taxed to the individual partners even though the money is not distributed.

This reinvestment has two advantages. First, the business can be built up with money which has been taxed only at the corporate rate and on which no individual shareholder needs to pay any tax. Second, the owner can delay the liquidation and distribution of corporate assets until a time of lower personal income and, therefore, lower tax liability. If, however, the amount withheld for expansion is unreasonably high, then the corporation may be exposed to a penalty. It is, therefore, wise to work with an experienced tax planner on a regular basis.

The S Corporation

Congress has created a hybrid organizational form, which allows the owners of a small corporation to take advantage of many of the features of incorporating, including limited liability, while avoiding the double taxation problem. This form of organization is called an S *corporation*. Income and losses flow directly to shareholders, and the corporation pays no income tax. This can be particularly advantageous in the early years of a corporation because the owners of an S corporation can deduct the losses of the corporation from their personal income, which is not permissible with a regular corporation (also called a C *corporation*). If the corporation is likely to sustain major losses, and shareholders have other sources of income against which they wish to write off those losses, the S corporation is probably a desirable form for the business.

"Small corporation" as defined by the tax law does not refer to the amount of business generated; rather, it refers to the number of owners. In order to qualify for S status, the corporation may not have more than seventy-five owners, each of whom must be either human beings who are U.S. citizens or resident aliens, or certain kinds of trusts or nonprofit corporations. Additionally, there cannot be more than one class of voting stock.

S corporations are generally taxed in the same way as partnerships, although, unfortunately, the tax rules for S corporations are not as simple as they are for partnerships. Generally speaking, however, the shareholder/owner of an S corporation can be taxed on his or her pro rata share of the distributable profits and may deduct his or her share of distributable losses.

LIMITED LIABILITY COMPANIES
One of the newest business forms is the limited liability company or LLC. This business form combines the limited liability features of a corporation with the tax advantages available to sole proprietors and partnerships, if desired. Although the first LLC statute was enacted in Wyoming in 1977, it did not become an attractive business form until 1988, when the Internal Revenue Service issued a ruling classifying the LLC as a partnership for tax purposes. In 1997, the Internal Revenue Code was amended to permit LLCs to elect to be taxed either like C corporations or like sole proprietors and partnerships. The LLC is now available in all states.

A craftsperson conducting business through an LLC can now shield his or her personal assets from the risks of the business in all situations except the individual's own wrongful acts. This liability shield is identical to that available through the corporate form. The owners of an LLC can also enjoy all of the tax advantages accorded to sole proprietors and partners, if desired.

LLCs do not have the same restrictions imposed on S corporations regarding the number of owners, the owner's citizenship status, and the type of owners (i.e., human beings or specified business forms). In fact, business corporations, partnerships, and other business forms can own interests in LLCs. LLCs may also have more than one class of voting units.

Most state LLC statutes permit the organization to be run by a single manager, if desired. Keep in mind that this business form is relatively new, so there is not yet any significant body of case law interpreting the meaning of the statutes permitting LLCs.

PRECAUTIONS FOR OWNERS OF MINORITY INTERESTS

Dissolving a corporation is not only painful because of certain tax penalties, but it is almost always impossible without the consent of the majority of the shareholders. This may be true of LLCs and LLPs as well. If you will be a minority owner of a business entity, you must realize that the majority will have ultimate and absolute control unless you, the minority owner, take certain precautions from the start. There are numerous horror stories of what majority owners have done to minority owners. Avoiding these problems is no more difficult than drafting an agreement among the owners. I recommend that you retain your own attorney to represent you during the company's formation rather than waiting until it is too late.

Additional discussion of corporate tax situations can be found in chapter 6.

2 CONTRACTS

Craftspeople have become more and more aware of the legal and practical problems that affect them as entrepreneurs. In this chapter, we will focus on one of the most fundamental of these—contracts. Clearly, we cannot cover the entire field of contract law, but perhaps I can help you become aware of some of the law's ramifications and enable you to see where you might need protection.

WHAT IS A CONTRACT?

A contract is defined as a legally binding promise or set of promises. The law requires the participants in a contract to perform the promises they have made to each other. In the event of nonperformance—usually called a *breach*—the law provides remedies to the injured party. For the purposes of this discussion, we will assume that the contract is between two people, although a contract may include several people and/or other entities.

The three basic elements of every contract are the *offer*, the *acceptance*, and the *consideration*.

Example: You show a potential customer a wooden bowl at a crafts fair and suggest that she buy it (the offer). The customer says she likes it and wants it (the acceptance). You agree on a price (the consideration). This is the basic framework, but a great many variations can be played on that theme.

TYPES OF CONTRACTS

Contracts may be *express* or *implied*; they may be *oral* or *written*. As discussed later in this chapter, there are some types of contracts, however, that *must* be in writing if they are to be legally enforceable.

Express Contracts

An *express* contract is one in which all the details are spelled out.

Example: You make a contract with a retail store to deliver two dozen wooden bowls, each twelve inches in diameter and made of walnut, that will be delivered on or before October 1st, at a price of $39.50 per bowl, to be paid for within thirty days of receipt of the merchandise.

That's fairly straightforward. If either party fails to live up to any material part of the contract, a breach has occurred, at which time the other party may withhold performance of his or her obligation until receiving assurance that the breaching party will perform. In the event that no such assurance is forthcoming, the injured party may have a *cause of action* and initiate a lawsuit for breach of contract.

If the bowls are delivered on October 15th but the store had advertised a wooden bowl sale for October 2nd, then time is an important consideration, and the store would not be required to accept the late shipment. If, however, time is not a material consideration, then the slight delay would probably be considered *substantial performance* and the store would have to accept the delivery.

Express contracts can be either oral or written, but if you are going to the trouble of expressing contractual terms, you should put your understanding in writing.

Implied Contracts

Implied contracts need not be very complicated, and they are usually not in writing.

Example: You call a supplier to order 100 pounds of clay without making any express statement that you will pay for the clay. The promise to pay is implied in the order and is enforceable when the clay is delivered.

With implied contracts, things can often become a lot stickier.

Example: An acquaintance asks you to bring over one of your new wall hangings to see how it will look in her living room. She asks if you would leave it with her for a few days. Two months later she still has it, and you overhear her raving to others about how marvelous it looks over the fireplace.

Is there an implied contract to purchase in this arrangement? That may depend on whether you are normally in the business of selling your work or whether you usually make loans or gifts of your work.

Most contracts into which craftspeople enter in connection with their work involve some aspect of the sale of that work: a direct sale to a customer, a consignment agreement with a dealer who will sell the work, or a commission to produce a work.

Let us examine the principles of offer, acceptance, and consideration in several situations for a hypothetical craftsproducer, Pat Smith.

Smith is a weaver who also teaches on a part-time basis. Smith has had numerous works accepted in local and regional exhibitions, has won several prizes, and has sold a good many woven wall hangings. In a word, Smith is developing quite a reputation as a promising fiber artist. With this brief background, we will look at the following situations and see whether an enforceable contract comes into existence.

- At a cocktail party, Jones expresses an interest in buying one of Smith's works. "It looks like your weavings will go up in price pretty soon," Jones tells Smith. "I'm going to buy one while I can still afford it."

   Is this a contract? If so, what are the terms of the offer? The particular work? The specific price? No, this is not really an offer that Smith can accept. It is nothing more than an opinion or a vague expression of intent.

- Brown offers to pay $400 for one of Smith's wall hangings that he saw in a show several months ago. At the show it was listed at $450, but Smith agrees to accept the lower price.

   Is this an enforceable contract? Yes! Brown has offered, in unambiguous terms, to pay a specific amount for a specific work, and Smith has accepted the offer. A binding contract exists.

- One day Jones shows up at Smith's studio and sees a particular wall hanging for which he offers $200. Smith accepts and promises to deliver it the next week, at which time Jones will pay for it. An hour later, Brown shows up. She likes the same wall hanging and offers Smith $300 for it. Can Smith accept the later offer?

   No—a contract exists with Jones. An offer was made and accepted. The fact that the object has not yet been delivered or paid for does not make the contract any less binding.

- Green discusses a commission he would like Smith to execute for a particular wall in his office. He offers to pay $600 if the work is satisfactory to him. Green approves preliminary sketches, and Smith completes the work. But when Smith shows up at Green's office to hang it, Green refuses to accept it because it does not satisfy him.

   Green is making the offer in this case, but the offer is conditional upon his satisfaction with the completed work. Smith can only accept the offer by producing something that meets Green's subjective standards—a risky business. There is no enforceable contract for payment until such time as Green indicates that the completed work is satisfactory.

Suppose, however, that Green came to Smith's studio and said that the completed work was satisfactory but, when Smith delivers it, says it does not look right on his office wall. This is too late for Green to change his mind. The contract became binding at the moment he indicated the work to be satisfactory. If he subsequently refuses to accept it, he would be breaching his contract.

Later in this chapter I mention that contracts for goods over $500 must be in writing. Under the Uniform Commercial Code, which governs contracts for the sale of goods, a commission to produce a work is a *personal-service* contract, as distinct from a contract for the sale of a piece already completed. Accordingly, the UCC generally does not apply to commissioned works, such as the one described here.

ORAL AND WRITTEN CONTRACTS

Contracts are enforceable only if they can be proven. The hypothetical examples mentioned above were oral contracts, and a great deal of detail is often lost in the course of remembering a conversation. The best practice, of course, is to get the deal in writing. The function of a written contract is not only to provide proof, but also to make very clear the understanding of the parties regarding the agreement and the terms of the contract.

Some artists and craftspeople are adamant about doing business strictly on the basis of so-called gentlemen's agreements, particularly with their galleries. The assumption seems to be that the best business relations are those based upon mutual trust. Some artists believe that any agreement other than a handshake belies this trust. Although there may be some validity to these assumptions, craftspeople would, nevertheless, be well advised to put all of their oral agreements into writing. Far too many craftspeople have suffered adverse consequences because of their reliance upon the sanctity of oral contracts.

Even in the best of business relationships, it is still possible that one or both parties might forget the terms of an oral agreement, or both parties might have quite different perceptions about the precise terms of the agreement. When, however, the agreement is put in writing, there is much less doubt as to the terms of the arrangement, although even a written contract may contain ambiguities if it is not carefully drafted. A written contract generally functions as a safeguard against subsequent misunderstanding or forgetfulness.

Perhaps the principal problem with oral contracts lies in the fact that they cannot always be proven or enforced. Proof of oral contracts typically centers around the conflicting testimony of the parties involved, and if neither party is able to establish by a preponderance of the evidence that his or her version of the contract is the correct one, then the oral contract may be considered nonexistent. The same result might occur if the parties cannot remember the precise terms of the agreement, which is often the case.

WHEN WRITTEN CONTRACTS ARE REQUIRED

Even if an oral contract is established, it may not always be enforceable. There are some agreements that the law requires to be in writing to be enforceable.

An early law that was designed to prevent fraud and perjury, known as the Statute of Frauds, provides that any contract that, by its terms, cannot be fully performed within one year must be in writing. This rule is narrowly interpreted, so if there is any possibility, no matter how remote, that the contract could be fully performed within one year, the contract need not be written.

For example, if a crafts artist agrees to submit one large work to a dealer each year for a period of five years, the contract would have to be in writing, since, by the very terms of the agreement, there is no way the contract could be performed within one year. If, on the other hand, the contract called for the artist to deliver five large works within a period of five years, the contract would not have to be in writing under the Statute of Frauds, since it is possible, though perhaps not probable, that the artist could deliver all five works within the first year. The fact that the crafts artist does not actually complete performance of the contract within one year is immaterial. So long as complete performance within one year is within the realm of possibility, the contract need not be in writing to be enforceable.

The Statute of Frauds further provides that any contract for the sale of goods for $500 or more is unenforceable unless it has been put in writing and signed by the party against whom the contract is sought to be enforced (i.e., the one that has breached the contract). The fact that a contract for a price in excess of $500 is not in writing does not void the agreement. The parties are free to perform the oral arrangement, but if one party refuses to perform, the other will be unable to legally enforce the agreement.

The law defines "goods" as all things that are *movable* at the time of making the contract, except for the money used as payment. There can be little doubt that the vast majority of craftswork or crafts supplies will be considered goods, so the real question here becomes whether a particular contract involves the sale of goods for a price of $500 or more. Although the answer would generally seem to be fairly clear, ambiguities can arise.

For example, if a supplier agrees to provide the craftsperson with all of his or her crafts-supply needs for the coming month, how is the price to be determined? Or if the artist sells a number of works to a dealer where the total purchase price exceeds $500, but the price of each individual work is less than $500, which price governs? In light of such ambiguities, it would seem that the safer course would be to put all oral agreements in writing.

NO-COST WRITTEN AGREEMENTS

At this point, craftspeople might object by asserting that they do not have the time, energy, or patience to draft contracts. After all, the business of the artist is the creation of art, not the formulation of written contracts steeped in legal jargon. Fortunately, the craftsperson will not always be required to do this, since the art supplier or retailer may be willing to draft a contract satisfactory to the artist. However, be wary of signing any form contracts—they will almost invariably be one-sided, with all the terms drafted in favor of whoever paid to have them drafted.

As a second alternative, the artist could employ an attorney to draft the contract. This may be worthwhile only when the contract involves a substantial transaction. With respect to smaller transactions, the legal fees may be much larger than the benefits derived from having a written contract.

The Uniform Commercial Code (UCC) provides craftspeople with a third, and perhaps the best, alternative. The UCC is a compilation of commercial laws for the sale of goods, enacted in some form in every state. By working within the UCC, craftspeople need not actually draft a contract or rely on anyone else to do so.

In situations where the UCC applies, it provides that, where both parties are merchants and one party sends the other a written confirmation of an oral contract within a reasonable time after that contract has been made, and the recipient does not object to the confirming memorandum within ten days of its receipt, then the contract will be deemed enforceable. Remember, however, that the UCC applies only to the sale of goods. It would, of course, be best for you to retain a copy of the written confirmation.

The law defines a *merchant* as any person who normally deals in goods of the kind that are sold or who, by his occupation, represents himself as having knowledge or skill peculiar to the practices or goods involved in the transaction. Thus, professional craftspeople and crafts dealers will be deemed merchants. Even an amateur artist will be considered a merchant, since adoption of the designation "potter" or "weaver" will be deemed as a representation of oneself as having special knowledge or skill in the field. The UCC rule will, therefore, apply to most oral contracts a craftsperson may make.

It should be emphasized that the sole effect of the confirming memorandum is that neither party can use the Statute of Frauds as a defense, assuming that the recipient fails to object within ten days after receipt of a confirming memorandum. The party sending the confirming memorandum still must prove that an oral contract was, in fact, made prior to, or at the same time as, the written confirmation. Once such proof is offered, neither party can raise the Statute of Frauds to avoid enforcement of the agreement.

The advantage of the confirming memorandum over a written contract lies in the fact that the confirming memorandum can be used without the active participation of the other contracting party. It would suffice, for example, to simply state: "This memorandum is to confirm our oral agreement." Since the artist would still have to prove the terms of that agreement, however, it would be useful to provide a bit more detail in the confirming memorandum, such as the subject of the contract, the date it was made, and the price or other consideration to be paid. Thus, the artist might draft something like the following:

> This memorandum is to confirm our oral agreement made on July 3, 2005, pursuant to which [artist] agreed to deliver to [dealer] on or before September 19, 2005, five pieces of pottery for the purchase price of $600.

The advantage of providing some detail in the confirming memorandum is twofold. First, in the event of a dispute, the craftsperson could introduce the memorandum as proof of the terms of the oral agreement. Second, the recipient of the memorandum will be precluded from offering any proof regarding the terms of the oral contract that contradicts the terms contained in the memorandum. The recipient or, for that matter, the party sending the memorandum can only introduce proof regarding the terms of the oral contract that are consistent with the terms, if any, found in the memorandum. Thus, the dealer in the above example could not claim that the contract called for the delivery of six pieces of pottery, because the quantity was stated and the dealer did not object. On the other hand, a dealer would be permitted to testify that the oral contract required the potter to package the pottery in a specific way, since this testimony would not be inconsistent with the terms stated in the memorandum.

One party to a contract can prevent the other from adding terms that are not spelled out in the confirming memorandum by ending the memorandum with a clause requiring all other terms to be contained in a written and signed document. Such a clause might read:

> This is the entire agreement between the parties and no modification, alteration or additional terms shall be enforceable unless in writing and signed by both parties.

If you use such a clause, be sure there are no additional agreed-to terms which have not been included in the written document, since a court will be confined to the "four corners" of the document when trying to determine what was agreed to between the parties. An exception to this rule is that a court may allow oral evidence for the purpose of interpreting ambiguities or explaining the meaning of certain technical terms. The court may also permit the parties to introduce evidence of past practices in connection with the contract in question, in connection with other agreements between the parties, or even in connection with similar contracts between other parties.

To summarize, craftspeople should not rely on oral contracts alone, since they offer little protection in the event of a dispute. The best protection is afforded by a written contract. It is a truism that oral contracts are not worth the paper on which they are written. If drafting a complete written contract proves too burdensome or costly, the craftsmaker should send the other party a memorandum confirming the oral agreement. This, at least, overcomes the initial barrier raised by the Statute of Frauds. Moreover, by recounting the terms in the memorandum, the craftsperson is in a much better position later on to prove the oral contract.

SUMMARY OF ESSENTIALS TO PUT INTO WRITING

A contract rarely need be—or should be—a long, complicated document written in legal jargon, designed to provide a handsome income to lawyers. Instead, a contract should spell out the terms of the agreement in simple language that both parties can understand.

At a minimum, a contract should include:

- The date of the agreement
- Identification of the parties
- A description of the goods being sold
- The price or other consideration
- The signatures of the parties*

To supplement these basics, the agreement should spell out whatever other terms might be applicable: pricing arrangements, payment schedules, insurance coverage, consignment details, and so forth.

Finally, it should be noted that a written document that leaves out essential terms of the contract presents many of the same problems of proof and ambiguity as an oral contract. Contract terms should be well conceived, clearly drafted, "conspicuous" (i.e., not in tiny print that is difficult to read), and in plain English so that everyone understands what the terms of the contract are.

---

*If you are signing on behalf of your corporation or other business entity, you should be sure to sign as follows:

[Business Name]
By: _____   _____
        Name: [You or Your Representative]   **Date**
        Its: [Title]

This is referred to as "signing in your corporate capacity," and failure to do so may subject you to the argument that you intended to personally guarantee the contract, thereby waiving any limited liability to which you might otherwise be entitled.

3
WARRANTIES
AND DISCLAIMERS

Craftspeople who sell their work, either directly or otherwise, may be warranting certain attributes of their work, whether they realize it or not. The rules that govern warranties have been embodied in legislation known as the Uniform Commercial Code (UCC). The Code, as mentioned in the preceding chapter, has been adopted in some form in all states.

A warranty is, in essence, a guarantee that the item sold will be of a certain quality or have particular attributes. There are a host of different warranties that apply to the sale of crafts objects. In this chapter, we will discuss warranties you may be giving without being aware of doing so, how to grant a specific warranty, and how to disclaim a warranty.

ELEMENTS OF AN EXPRESS WARRANTY

Any factual statement or promise that describes an item will create what is known in legal language as an *express warranty*. In general, you do not need to use the words "warrant" or "guarantee" to create an express warranty. However, the more explicit your statement, the more likely it is that you have given an express warranty.

In order to determine whether a craftsperson, during a sale, has made statements of the type which will give rise to an express warranty or are merely expressions of opinion, the courts have developed a test. If the seller makes a statement that relates to the goods and about some factor of which the buyer is ignorant, that statement is probably an express warranty. On the other hand, if the seller merely expresses a judgment about something on which each party would be expected to have an opinion, no express warranty is created. For example, if a potter states that a bowl is oven-safe, this statement would likely be considered an express warranty since the creator would be more likely to know about the qualities of the specific pot than would the buyer, who knew only about pottery in general.

To further determine whether or not a statement will be considered an express warranty, a number of factors are relevant. A written statement, particularly if it is part of a contract or bill of sale, is more likely to be considered an express warranty than is an oral statement. How much the seller qualifies the statement is also an indication as to whether or not an express warranty is created; generally, the more qualifications, the more likely an express warranty.

Another way an express warranty can be created is by giving a description of the crafts object, which description is part of the basis of the bargain or sale. The description does not need to be the sole inducement to the buyer to purchase the goods. To create a warranty, any representations must be part of the contract or sale negotiation, but the precise timing of the statement is irrelevant. The buyer could already have paid for an item and the seller could then make a statement that could be considered as part of the basis of the bargain since, theoretically, the buyer could still decide to return the goods to the seller and obtain a refund. However, these post-purchase statements must be made within a reasonable period of time to be considered part of the bargain, and they probably only apply in face-to-face dealings. An additional problem is presented if you sell your crafts either through a catalog or advertisements. Catalogs or advertisements, and any statements made in them, could be considered part of the basis of the bargain, although buyers would probably have to prove they relied on the statements contained in the catalog or advertisement if the statement is to be used for that purpose.

An express warranty can also be created by the use of samples or models. There is a distinction between a sample and a model. A sample is one of the objects actually being sold. Therefore, the sample "describes" the qualities of the goods being sold, unless the seller specifically states otherwise. For instance, if you show a customer one handwoven placemat from a group of eight and the customer does not investigate the other seven, an express warranty is created that the remaining seven are of similar color, size, and composition as the one seen by the customer. A model, on the other hand, might not be from the exact group of goods which are the subject of the sale. A model is not quite as descriptive as a sample, but an express warranty can still be created.

If you take an order based on a sample or model and want to give an express warranty, the following language could be used:

> Seller warrants that the goods, when delivered, shall conform to the sample/model that was exhibited to buyer on [date] by [name] (the sales representative of seller) at [address].

If you are making a sale of many items, such as 200 wooden toys, based on a sample or model, and the buyer wants all the toys to be similar, you might want to make the following warranty:

> Seller warrants that the goods shall be without variation, except that caused by the individual creation of each piece, and shall be of uniform kind, quality, and quantity within each unit and among all units of the goods covered in this agreement.

IMPLIED WARRANTIES

In addition to express warranties, the UCC provides for a number of *implied* warranties that are presumed to be part of the sales transaction.

Implied Warranty of Merchantability

The implied warranty of merchantability applies whenever the seller is a *merchant.* "Merchants" are defined as people who deal with goods of the kind involved in the sale, or who, by their occupation, hold themselves out as having particular knowledge or skill. For example, a professional craftsworker would be considered a merchant because of having held him- or herself out as having special knowledge or skills with regard to a craft. A merchant can also be one to whom this knowledge or skill can be attributed because he or she is acting as an agent for a merchant.

Some of the considerations in defining *merchantability* are:

- Does the item pass without objection under the description given in the contract?
- Is the item at least fit for the ordinary purposes for which such goods are used?
- Does the item at least conform to the promises or affirmations of fact made on the container or label, if any?
- Is the item of average quality, based on the description given?
- Does the item fall within the variations permitted by the agreement between the parties?

- Are the items of an even kind, quality, and quantity within each unit and among units?

Be aware that to be merchantable, an item need not be perfect. *Trade usage*, that is, the norms of a particular trade, will also establish the particular qualities that will be acceptable for items produced by members of that trade. Generally, the higher an item is priced, the more justifiable the buyer's expectations of high quality.

Craftspeople should be aware of the implied warranty of merchantability they are creating when they sell their goods. For instance, a fiber artist who creates handcrafted hammocks is warranting that they will withstand ordinary usage, probably including use by a heavy adult or an energetic child.

An express warranty of fitness for ordinary purpose is created as follows:

> Seller warrants that the goods shall be fit for the purpose for which such goods are ordinarily intended.

Implied Warranty of Fitness for a Particular Purpose

When a seller knows of a particular purpose for which the buyer is purchasing the goods and knows the buyer is relying on the seller to choose suitable goods, there is an implied warranty that the goods will fit that purpose. This warranty is referred to as *fitness for a particular purpose*. The usual way this warranty is created is by the buyer asking the seller for assistance.

Example: If an individual comes to you and requests assistance in choosing a handwoven bedspread for a baby, an implied warranty is created which would probably include at least three specific attributes: the bedspread is not made out of any toxic materials, so the baby can safely put it in her mouth; it is made from non-flammable materials; and it can be washed without running or shrinking, unless you specifically tell the buyer it must be drycleaned or handwashed. Similarly, in the case of children's toys and furniture, sellers implicitly warrant that the items do not contain toxic substances such as lead-based paint.

Fitness for a particular purpose requires a product to be specifically suitable for the buyer's use. A crafted object purchased because it esthetically pleases the buyer probably is not serving a *particular* purpose but, instead, an *ordinary* purpose. A particular purpose must be reasonably specific for the seller to be held to have been informed of the buyer's purpose. If a potential purchaser asks for advice, it would behoove you to ask that person specifically what attributes are desired so you can give good advice and not find yourself later on with an unhappy purchaser whose desires you misunderstood.

If the buyer is knowledgeable about your craft, it is less likely that this form of implied warranty is created.

The one exception to this warranty is when a buyer asks for a particular brand or a particular craftsperson's product. In that case, the buyer is not relying on the seller's skill and judgment, so no implied warranty of fitness for a particular purpose is created.

Implied Warranty of Title

A warranty of title is implied in every contract for sale of goods. This simply means that the seller has good title (the right to sell the item) and that the seller is unaware of any outstanding lien or other encumbrance against the item. This warranty is unlikely to create problems when craftspeople sell their own goods.

It is unlikely that you would ever need to give an express warranty of title unless you were acting as a broker for other craftspersons and your buyer wanted a guarantee that you owned all the items you were selling. In that case, you could use the following language:

> Seller warrants and represents that seller has absolute and good title to, and the right to dispose of _____, and that there are no liens, claims or encumbrances of any kind against the goods.

The blank would be filled in with a description of the goods being sold.

If for any reason there might be encumbrances against one of your works and you wish to assure the buyer that the encumbrance will be removed when the item is delivered, you might want to make the following warranty:

> Seller warrants that the goods shall be delivered free of any security interest or other lien or encumbrance.

This warranty states that by the time you deliver the item, it will no longer be subject to a lien. If you make this warranty, you *must*, before delivery, satisfy all lienholders who are holding a security interest or claim against the particular item or you will breach this warranty. If it is not possible to extinguish all liens, then you must list those which remain as exceptions to the above warranty. That is, your warranty should read:

Seller warrants that the goods shall be delivered free of any security interest or other lien or encumbrance, except for the following: [list]

Implied Warranty against Infringement

The most modern of the implied warranties is the *implied warranty against infringement*. When a crafts product is sold, the seller warrants that the item is not infringing any rights protected by patent, trademark, copyright or trade dress. If a crafts object was created in violation of a copyright holder's intellectual property rights, that warranty has been breached. For instance, if you copied a sculptor's copyrighted work and sold it, you would have breached this implied warranty. The sculptor could sue the purchaser, and the purchaser could sue you.

If you want to provide an implied warranty against infringement expressly because the buyer requests that you do so, the following language can be used:

Seller warrants that the goods shall be delivered free of the rightful claim of any person arising from patent, copyright, trademark, or trade dress infringement.

Not only does this implied warranty extend from seller to buyer, it may also go in the other direction—from the buyer to the seller. For example, if a person comes to you and requests that you make him a wooden statue, shows you a picture of what he wants and gives you the dimensions, the buyer is warranting that the item he is having you create will not infringe upon anyone else's work. If you are sued for infringement, the buyer must hold you harmless from any claims. To protect yourself from potential problems when a person asks you to create a specific item, it would be wise if you asked the buyer where the idea came from and, if possible, to tell you whether the item is protected or not. You might also want to explain what liability the buyer might face if infringing on someone else's rights.

DISCLAIMING A WARRANTY

What can you do if you do not want to give one or more of these express or implied warranties? You can use disclaimers, but the UCC provides certain methods for providing effective ones.

To be safe, disclaimers should be in writing. When you have already given an express warranty, it is quite difficult to disclaim it, since the law considers it unreasonable to give an express warranty and then turn around and disclaim it. An attempt to disclaim an express warranty will usually not be effective. This includes any express warranties that may be set forth in a description of an item. Also, you cannot limit the time period within which the buyer must discover the breach of the warranty. You may, however, give an express warranty in writing and exclude all *implied* warranties. You should say:

> The above warranty is in lieu of any other warranty, express or limited, including but not limited to any implied warranty of merchantability or fitness for a particular purpose, which warranties are expressly excluded.

Disclaiming a Salesperson's Statements

A fairly common problem occurs when a customer claims that oral warranties were made prior to the signing of a written contract. The seller may be shielded from this problem by the rule that sometimes prevents prior oral statements from being considered as part of the contract. However, there are exceptions of which you should be aware.

If there is a written agreement and it is not final, the written agreement will not overcome prior oral express warranties. Also, if the oral terms are consistent with a written disclaimer, the oral terms will be considered if the writing was not intended as a complete and exclusive statement. These types of problems tend to arise when someone else sells your goods for you. If you often have a sales representative or friend sell your goods, you would be wise to include a limitation of the salesperson's authority on any written receipt or bill of sale (which is considered a contract).

If you use the following disclaimer, it should appear clearly on the face—not the back—of any receipt.

> The salesperson may have made oral statements about the merchandise described in the bill of sale. The salesperson has no authority to make any such representations and, if made, such statements do not constitute warranties, should not be relied upon by the buyer, and are not part of the contract for sale. The entire contract is embodied in this writing. This writing constitutes the final expression of the parties' agreement, and it is a complete and exclusive statement of the terms of that agreement.

If you have a commission agreement, consignment agreement or some other longer written agreement that includes sections describing the crafts item and might be misconstrued as a warranty by the buyer, you might want to include the following:

> Unless a statement in this agreement is specifically identified as a warranty, the statements made in this agreement by the seller relating to _____ are not warranties and do not form part of the basis of the bargain, but are made merely in the course of the negotiations of the parties.

The blank should be filled in with a description of the subject matter of the agreement, e.g., "the Work," "the Picture," "the Sculpture."

Disclaimers for Models and Samples

If you want to make a disclaimer after showing a customer a model or sample, the following could be used. This disclaimer must be given at the time the order is taken or the sale is made; it is not sufficient to send it with the goods when they are delivered to the buyer.

> The model [sample] shown by seller to buyer is used for demonstration purposes only. There is no warranty that the goods as delivered shall conform to the model [sample], and conformity of the goods to the model [sample] is not part of the basis of the bargain between seller and buyer.

Disclaiming All Warranties

Implied warranties can also be disclaimed. If you want to disclaim all warranties, express and implied, the following language should be used:

> *Exclusion of Warranties.* The parties agree that the implied warranties of merchantability, fitness for a particular purpose, and title and all other warranties, express or implied, are excluded from this transaction and do not apply to the goods sold.

The implied warranty of title can be disclaimed only by specific language or by circumstances which give the buyer reason to know that the seller does not have title or is only selling the title he has, which is subject to a third party's interest.

Specifically excluding the warranty of title may cause the prospective purchaser to question your business principles. Therefore, this disclaimer should not be made unless absolutely necessary. If you must disclaim this warranty, the following language softens the effect. The entire second sentence should be omitted if you have any question about your title to the item.

> Seller makes no warranty as to the title to the goods, and buyer assumes all risks of seller's nonownership of the goods. Seller does warrant that, at the time of signing this agreement, seller neither knows of, nor has reason to know of, the existence of any title or claim of title to the goods hostile to the rights of seller.

To exclude or modify the implied warranty of merchantability, the word "merchantability" must be specifically mentioned and the disclaimer must be conspicuous. This warranty can be disclaimed orally, but the implied warranty of fitness for a particular purpose can be disclaimed only in writing.

The implied warranty against infringement can also be disclaimed. If you create a work on commission based on the buyer's description, even though this implied warranty extends from buyer to seller as well as vice versa, inserting this disclaimer in any sales documents will provide further protection for you.

> Seller has no knowledge as to trademark, copyright, trade dress, or patent rights which third parties may claim in the goods. Consequently, seller makes no warranty whatsoever with respect to the freedom of said goods from claims of infringement of third parties arising from trademark, copyright, trade dress, patent, or other property rights in said goods.

Making a Disclaimer Conspicuous

If you are going to disclaim a warranty, you must do so conspicuously, so that a reasonable person ought to have noticed the disclaimer. Methods commonly used to make a disclaimer conspicuous in a document include use of a different typeface, a different color, or larger print. A disclaimer will not be considered conspicuous by a court if there is only a slight contrast with the rest of the document or if only the heading is in a different typeface or color.

Cases Where Written Disclaimers Might Not Be Necessary

Warranties can be disclaimed by means other than a written document. The most common method is the phrase "as is" or "with all faults" on a tag attached to the item. These statements will exclude all implied warranties and are most likely to be found on used goods or new goods with obvious faults. The statement "as is" must be conspicuous, and the buyer must understand what is meant by that phrase. A phrase that has come into common usage in recent years is "as found." This is most typically applied to items in antique and thrift stores. The term is not found in the Uniform Commercial Code but its growing popularity will likely aid sellers in establishing the "as is" nature of the item.

If the buyer has had an opportunity to examine the item as much as desired or has refused to examine an item after having been given an opportunity to do so, no implied warranty has been created as to defects which the examination ought to have revealed. Mere availability for inspection is insufficient, however, if the buyer has not been encouraged to inspect the item.

The difficulty with relying on this type of disclaimer is that it will not apply if the buyer is ignorant of the attributes of your craft. As indicated earlier in this chapter, examination of your crafts object or a sample or model can create express warranties, and it is better to use a written disclaimer than to depend on the buyer discovering a defect.

To clarify your position and protect yourself from future claims arising after delivery, you could make the following disclaimer:

> Buyer acknowledges that he/she is making this purchase after and in complete reliance upon her/his full and entire inspection of the goods to be sold hereunder and not by reason of any representation made by or on behalf of seller as to the merchantability, specific attributes, or otherwise of said goods.

Warranties can also be disclaimed if there have been prior dealings between the parties. If you have previously dealt with a buyer and not given a warranty, a warranty should not be expected in subsequent deals. For example, if you regularly provide a restaurant with pottery mugs and have previously disclaimed a warranty against chipping under ordinary use and care, the restaurant cannot come back to you later and allege a breach of warranty for chipped mugs.

In a similar manner, trade usage also makes it possible to disclaim a warranty. Trade usage is any practice so regularly observed in a business or trade that an expectation is created that will apply to particular situations. If a certain kind of pottery is generally not ovenproof, no implied warranty can require that a particular casserole be ovenproof. For this type of disclaimer to apply, the applicable trade usage must be understood by both parties. This again presupposes that your buyer is familiar with the attributes of your craft.

It would be wise to not put much reliance on these last two kinds of disclaimers, because they depend for their effectiveness on an informed buyer. It would be safer to specifically disclaim any warranties in writing.

A craftsperson is well advised to consult with an attorney to determine which warranties should be disclaimed and the best method of accomplishing this. The rules on disclaimers are quite technical, and care should be taken to determine how much risk you may have in a particular situation.

FEDERAL RULES REGARDING WARRANTIES AND DISCLAIMERS

If you decide to give a written warranty or written disclaimer of warranty, you should be aware that there are federal regulations promulgated under the Magnuson-Moss Act to cover consumer products. According to this act, the following items must be indicated in a written warranty:

- To whom the warranty is extended
- Exactly what parts of the product are covered
- What the warrantor will do in case of a defect
- When the warranty begins and ends
- What the buyer has to do to get warranty coverage
- Any limitation on the duration of implied warranties (this is not allowed in some states)
- Any exclusions or limitations regarding relief

In the written warranty, you must also specify what you are promising regarding the material and workmanship and specify that the item is defect-free or will meet a specific level of performance. You must also clearly indicate whether the warranty is full or limited. Under a full warranty, the warrantor agrees to:

- Repair the product within a reasonable period of time without charge if the product has a defect, malfunctions or fails to conform to the written warranty
- Not impose a limitation on implied warranties
- Not exclude or limit consequential damages (unless this is already clear on the face of the warranty)
- Replace the item or refund the purchase price if the item is unsuccessfully repaired numerous times

If any one of the above qualifications is not met, you have given a limited warranty.

If you breach a warranty and the buyer is damaged by your failure to comply with the warranty obligations, the buyer may sue and, if successful, receive damages, as well as court costs and reasonable attorney fees. Since these remedies exist, you should be careful to determine which warranties you are giving and learn how to disclaim those you do not want to give.

A craftsperson should discuss with a business lawyer the extent of exposure that may be expected as a result of the numerous warranties applying to the sale of a crafts object. Warranty disclaimers, as well as limitations of liability, can be used to reduce your exposure, but skilled drafting is necessary for effective protection. As an alternative or supplement for an ineffective disclaimer, you might want to purchase product liability insurance as a means of insulating yourself from extensive liability.

AUTHENTICITY OF A LIMITED EDITION

Several states (including California, Georgia, Hawaii, Illinois, Maryland, Michigan, Minnesota, New York, North Carolina, Oregon, and South Carolina) have enacted laws that require disclosure certificates to accompany the sale of limited-edition prints and other multiples, such as limited-edition sculptures. The purpose of these laws is to overcome many of the abuses that have occurred in the limited-edition market. If your craft is created in a limited edition and you wish to use a certificate, see appendix C(1) for a form. You should also check with an attorney to determine whether states other than those described above in which you will be selling your work have enacted so-called multiples laws, as well.

CONSUMER PROTECTION LAWS

The federal government and many states have enacted legislation designed to give consumers the opportunity to change their minds and cancel an unwanted sale. The federal law generally applies to any sale, loan, or rental of consumer goods or services which has a purchase price of $25 or more in which the seller, or the seller's representative, personally solicits the sale and the buyer's agreement or offer to purchase is made at a place other than the seller's place of business. The "place of business of the seller" is defined as the main or permanent branch office or local address of the seller.

Cooling-off Period for Field Sales

These laws protect the consumer by offering a cooling-off period within which to notify the seller of an intention to cancel the purchase. The consumer may receive a return of all money paid and rescind any contract signed without further obligation. In effect, the consumer is given a period of time, typically up to midnight of the third business day following the sale, during which to determine whether he or she really wants to go through with the transaction.

The seller's principal obligation under these regulations is to disclose to the potential consumer that such a cooling-off period exists and that it is the consumer's right to take advantage of that escape clause and cancel the sale if desired. The form and content of this disclosure requirement is spelled out in the federal regulations.

To comply with the statute, a seller must be prepared to furnish the buyer with a fully completed receipt or copy of any agreement pertaining to the sale at the time the sale is made or the agreement is signed. The receipt or agreement must be in the same language that was predominately used in the oral sales presentation. That is, if the presentation were made in Spanish, the receipt or agreement must also be in Spanish. It also must include the seller's name and address, time and date of sale, and a statement on the first page that contains the following language:

> You, the buyer, may cancel this transaction at any time prior to midnight of the third business day after the date of this transaction. See the attached notice-of-cancellation form for an explanation of this right.

The notice-of-cancellation form must detail the buyer's rights and obligations in the event the buyer chooses to cancel the sale.

In addition to the federal regulation, many states have enacted similar consumer protection statutes that provide for a cooling-off period and contain a similar disclosure requirement. It is strongly advised that if you engage in consumer sales other than from a permanently established business location, you confer with an attorney who can advise you of the legal requirements in your particular state.

MAIL-ORDER SALES

Popular methods of selling today are through a mail-order service or catalog sales and over the Internet. Here, too, the federal government has established certain guidelines aimed at protecting the consuming public.

When a seller solicits a sale through the Internet or a mail-order catalog, the seller must reasonably expect to be able to ship any ordered merchandise to the buyer within the time stated in the solicitation, or within thirty days after receiving a properly completed order if no time period is stated. If the seller is unable to ship the merchandise within the specified time limit, the seller must offer the buyer the option of either consenting to a delay in shipping or canceling the order and receiving a prompt refund. The seller is also required to inform the buyer of any anticipated delays in shipping and to explain why the shipping deadline cannot be met.

4 CONSIGNMENT

One of the more difficult aspects of being a craftsperson is selling your work. Many craftsworkers find this part of their profession to be a bit too mundane to warrant much time or consideration, but the fact remains that craftsworkers generally sell their work. Those who are unable or unwilling to market their works are usually compelled to seek other employment, which detracts from the time they could otherwise spend as professional craftsmakers.

There are three basic ways by which craftspeople sell their work: (1) *direct sales*, typically at crafts shows, their own retail shops, or craft mall spaces; (2) *wholesale* to department stores, boutiques, museum shops, and the like; and (3) *consignment*, usually through galleries, but often through other retail outlets. Many craftspeople sell their work via a combination of all three methods.

Working on large commissions or selling through agents is another sales method, but this is generally available only to more successful or prolific craftspeople. For a form that may be used when work is to be commissioned, see appendix C(2).

Outright sales to customers and wholesalers are fairly matter-of-fact situations, at least as far as the legal ramifications are concerned. One party sells, the other party buys, and money changes hands at the time the goods are transferred (or shortly thereafter). When the goods leave the seller's possession, they become the property of the buyer.

Consignment selling can be quite a bit more complicated. Under a typical consignment arrangement, the craftsperson (the *consignor*) delivers his or her work to a gallery or other dealer (the *consignee*). The consignee does not make an outright purchase of the work, but rather, agrees to remit to the consignor the proceeds from sales less the consignment commission as the sales are made. Generally, the consignee is under no obligation to sell the goods and may return them to the consignor at any time. For a sample consignment agreement, see appendix C(2).

ADVANTAGES OF CONSIGNMENT

Although it may not be immediately obvious, a consignment arrangement can be beneficial to both parties. For the gallery, consignments eliminate much of the financial risks of purchasing works of questionable market appeal. If the work does not sell or sells poorly, the gallery will generally not lose much money, since it has made no direct investment by purchasing the pieces. The gallery loses only to the extent that the display space was filled by that consignment work when it could have been filled by other pieces having greater sales potential, along with whatever amount of money was expended on advertising, overhead, and the like.

The advantage to the craftsworker is that consignment provides an opportunity to get a work into retail outlets where it might not otherwise be accepted. This is particularly true for the work of unknown craftspeople, who often find that this is the only way they can prove their work will sell. Another advantage is that the craftsworker generally gets a larger share of the retail-selling price (around 60 percent in consignment versus 50 percent in wholesaling—although that is changing, and consignment percentages are getting closer and closer to the 50 percent wholesale arrangement).

DISADVANTAGES OF CONSIGNMENT

There are, however, several deterrents that often make craftspeople reluctant to engage in consignment selling. After all, it is the craftsperson who takes most of the risks in such arrangements. Some of the questions that are bound to occur are: How promptly will the consignee pay after the work is sold? Is the work insured while it is on the consignee's premises? Will unsold work be returned in good condition? How much paperwork and recordkeeping will be involved?

Other deterrents to the consignment arrangement are more complicated. What happens, for example, if a craftsperson puts his or her work in a gallery on consignment and the gallery subsequently goes bankrupt? Or, what if the gallery fails to pay debts to a creditor who has a security interest in the gallery's assets? Would the security interest cover the consigned work? The resolution of these questions depends upon a determination of which party—the craftsworker on the one hand or the creditor or bankruptcy trustee on the other—has "priority" over the consigned work. There is no question that all of these parties may have valid claims to the work; the issue is, rather, whose claims are to be given first priority.

IF A CONSIGNEE GOES BANKRUPT

Before the enactment of the Uniform Commercial Code, the craftsmaker/ consignor would generally prevail over the consignee/gallery's creditors or the consignee's trustee in bankruptcy with respect to the consigned work. Moreover, the craftsworker would prevail, even if there were no record of the consignment enabling the consignee to give creditors or a trustee in bankruptcy notice of the consignment's existence. In effect, the craftsperson held a secret lien on the consigned work that was given priority over all other liens.

However, the UCC revised the rule of priority largely in response to the general consensus that secret liens should not be legally enforceable. Thus, Article 2 of the UCC provides that where a craftsperson delivers work to a business dealing in goods of that kind, such as a gallery, the craftsworker will not have priority over the claims of creditors or a trustee in bankruptcy unless the craftsworker does one of three things:

(1) Complies with the applicable state law providing that the consignor's interest be evidenced by a sign on the goods
(2) Establishes in court that the consignee is known by his or her creditors to be substantially engaged in selling goods under consignment
(3) Complies with the filing requirements in Article 9 of the UCC

As to the first option, most states do not have sign laws. Even in those states that do, the consignor should not rely on the consignee to place and maintain a sign on the goods indicating that they have been consigned, since it may not be in the interest of the consignee to do so. For example, a gallery would generally be in a much better position to obtain loans if a lending institution were led to believe that all of the work in the gallery was owned outright, as opposed to being consigned.

Additionally, the consignor should not expect to prevail under the second option since it will generally be difficult to prove that the consignee was known by its creditors to be substantially engaged in the business of selling consigned goods. This problem is made somewhat easier for the craftsworker by the fact that many galleries in the United States sell their works on consignment. Nevertheless, the craftsworker would be ill advised to rely exclusively on this option as a means of protecting his or her work. Merely pointing to customary practices in the crafts world may not be sufficient to meet the craftsperson's burden of proof.

This leaves the third option. As a general rule, the craftsworker can best protect his or her consigned work by complying with the filing provisions contained in Article 9 of the UCC. The purpose of this filing requirement is simply to give notice to interested parties that certain property is subject to outstanding interests. The filing requirement gives notice to creditors, lending institutions, and the like that the work within the gallery is subject to a consignment agreement between the gallery and the craftsperson.

This process is a complicated, time-consuming exercise that requires the filing of financing statements with the Secretary of State in every state where the consigned work is located, paying filing fees each time, and giving notice to the consignee's creditors, as well as meeting several other requirements.

There has been considerable debate as to whether the UCC provisions adequately safeguard the craftsworker's interests under consignment arrangements. As an initial consideration, there is the problem that craftspeople may not even be aware that the protection exists. Unlike consignors in other fields, artists and craftspeople are not always sophisticated in the ways of business and law. Moreover, even if the craftsperson knows the protection exists, he or she may be unable or unwilling to learn how that protection can be secured. In terms of complying with the filing requirements of Article 9, many craftspeople who know what is needed may find that this approach is too complex and bothersome.

SPECIFIC LAWS COVERING CONSIGNMENT

As a result of these problems and others, many states have enacted special artist-gallery consignment laws. The first of these was enacted by New York in 1966. Subsequently, similar legislation was passed in thirty other states: Alaska, Arizona, Arkansas, California, Colorado, Connecticut, Florida, Georgia, Idaho, Illinois, Iowa, Kentucky, Maryland, Massachusetts, Michigan, Minnesota, Missouri, Montana, New Hampshire, New Jersey, New Mexico, North Carolina, Ohio, Oregon, Pennsylvania, Rhode Island, Tennessee, Texas, Washington, and Wisconsin. Other states are considering such laws, largely in response to pressure from artists and arts organizations.

Although each state has enacted a unique version, the basic provisions of artist-gallery consignment laws are essentially the same. Most statutes provide that any works of art delivered to any art dealer are presumed to be delivered under a consignment arrangement unless the artist has been paid in full on or before delivery. Thus, the majority of transactions between artists and various art dealers will be deemed consignments for purposes of these statutes.

In addition, most artist-gallery consignment statutes provide that the art dealer holds all consigned artwork, as well as the proceeds derived from the sale of the artwork, in trust for the benefit of the artist. This basically means that the art dealer will be solely responsible for any loss, theft, or damage to the consigned artwork that could have been avoided had the art dealer exercised the utmost care and caution. Many statutes go so far as to impose strict liability upon the dealer for loss or damage, i.e., the art dealer will be liable even though such loss or damage could not have been avoided by exercise of the utmost care and caution.

Several of these laws require the artist and the dealer to enter into a written contract containing at least the following information: the value of the artwork, the minimum price for which it may be sold, and the percentage to be paid to the dealer. Additional issues that may be addressed include the duration of the consignment relationship, who assumes the costs for shipping and storage, the payment schedule for the craftsperson, and the extent and nature of marketing and promotion to be done by the dealer. The protective provisions of consignment legislation cannot be waived. Accordingly, any attempt to avoid these provisions by contract is prohibited by law.

Finally, and perhaps most importantly, nearly all of these statutes provide that the consigned artwork is protected against claims asserted by the art dealer's creditors, including a trustee in bankruptcy. Thus, at least one effect of the consignment legislation is to provide artists with similar protection to that afforded by Article 9 of the UCC without requiring the artist to take any steps to procure that protection. (See the section on gallery bankruptcy in chapter 5 for additional information.)

CRAFTSWORKS: COVERED OR NOT?

Although art consignment legislation would seem to solve many of the practical problems of consignments, the craftsperson as artist should review how the applicable legislation, if any, defines the terms "art dealer" and "artwork." Fortunately for the craftsperson, "art dealer" has been broadly defined by nearly all states as being any person engaged in the business of selling artwork other than a person exclusively engaged in selling goods at public auction.

On the other hand, artwork has sometimes been given a rather narrow definition. A few statutes have defined artwork as encompassing only the traditional areas of fine art, such as paintings, sculptures, drawings, and the like. This means that under some consignment statutes, the product of many craftspeople may not be deemed to be within the purview of the statutory protection. Fortunately, most statutes expressly include craftsworks such as those made of clay, fiber, wood, metal, plastic, or glass as being within the definition of a work of art protected by the legislation.

Whether the exclusion of crafts from some consignment legislation was merely an oversight or a reflection of the long-standing, though unwarranted, notion that crafts are somehow inferior to the traditional fine arts is not clear. In any event, people engaged in the various crafts would do well to form or support cohesive lobbying organizations and, thereby, strengthen their power with state legislators. If enough pressure were placed upon legislators, existing statutes could be amended to include crafts within their protection, and new legislation could be drafted to include crafts within the scope of protected works.

EXCLUSIVITY

Craftspeople should carefully consider the important issue of exclusivity when entering into a consignment arrangement. Unless the craftsperson is a powerhouse in the field, there is likely to be a disparity in bargaining power between the craftsperson and the dealer. A craftsperson may be intimidated into agreeing to an exclusive arrangement.

There are two types of exclusivity: exclusive agency and exclusive power to sell. If the dealer is the exclusive agent of the craftsperson, the craftsperson can sell works independently and not be liable to the dealer for a commission. If the exclusivity arrangement is for the power to sell, the craftsperson who independently sells a work is liable to the dealer for a commission and may be in breach of contract.

There is a question about exclusivity as applied to "bartering" situations as well. If you, as craftsmaker, exchange your vase for the use of a condominium, is your exclusive agent (the dealer) entitled to a commission? Art dealers usually interpret exclusive arrangements broadly, but the craftsperson's interpretation may be quite different.

Exclusivity carries both positive and negative aspects. The gallery dealer benefits by being the only agent for the craftsmaker, thereby generating business, particularly if the craftsmaker is or becomes well known and appreciated. In return, the dealer believes that the craftsmaker benefits because the gallery promotes the artist as well as his or her works. Craftsmakers, on the other hand, may see an exclusive arrangement as too restrictive. An exclusive arrangement that binds the two together reduces the freedom of the craftsmaker to pursue other sales avenues. Also, if minimum sales are not guaranteed, the craftsmaker is not assured a return under an exclusive arrangement. He or she, at that point, will still be unable to go outside of the arrangement to sell his or her works.

You, as a craftsworker, should consider the following factors when faced with the decision of entering into an exclusivity contract: Is there direct competition between the galleries you are interested in dealing with? Is the gallery owner willing to guarantee a minimum amount in sales? Is your line diverse enough to be shown in more than one gallery in a given geographic area?

As a craftsworker, you should carefully consider the pluses and minuses of an exclusive dealer arrangement. Its impact on the marketing of your work is the key consideration.

5
ON GETTING PAID FOR YOUR WORK

It is axiomatic that craftspeople who sell their work must wear two hats—as craftspeople and as businesspeople. This may be distasteful to some, but it is, nevertheless, necessary if you want to realize the fruit of your labors.

COLLECTION PROBLEMS

It can be difficult enough to make a sale—either directly to the ultimate client or consumer, or through a retail store or gallery. In either case, collection problems can and do occur. There are several methods to deal with these problems, ranging from preventive action to initiating a lawsuit.

The general rule in a sales transaction is that payment is due upon delivery of the item being sold. While this rule may be subject to some technical complications beyond the scope of this discussion, it means that when work is delivered to a customer, the seller has the legal right to demand payment in full at that moment. This assumes that no arrangement has been made between the buyer and the seller that would allow the purchaser to delay payment.

While payment upon delivery is common in retail transactions, it is unusual when selling through a dealer or gallery. In addition, the purchase of a rather expensive item may be subject to an installment sale arrangement.

If you are fortunate enough to deal with people who always pay their bills on time, then the remaining portion of this chapter may be of no concern to you. If, however, you have experienced delays in payment, or have had some totally uncollectible bills, then the suggestions that follow should prove useful.

POINT-OF-SALE PAYMENTS

Craftspeople who deal directly with the public at crafts shows, fairs, or at their own retail spaces customarily expect to be paid at the moment they make the sale, before the craftswork is taken away by the customer. Such payment is made by cash, check, or debit or credit card. It is, therefore, necessary for the craftsperson to determine whether the currency is authentic, whether the check is going to be paid by the bank, or whether the credit card will be honored.

Currency

Identifying counterfeit currency can be very technical and difficult. It is fairly simple if the counterfeiter has made a glaring error, such as using George Washington on a $5 bill, but subtle irregularities are more likely the norm. The federal government is quite diligent in alerting business-people to the presence of counterfeit currency in a particular area when it is aware of the problem. The introduction of newly designed currency has made it much easier for the seller to identify many counterfeit bills, by use of an inexpensive marking pen designed for this purpose. The best way to avoid being stuck with a counterfeit bill continues to be to keep your eyes open. It is not a good idea to accept any bills larger than $50.

Debit and Credit Cards

To avoid card fraud, the first thing to do is to compare the signature on the back of the card with the signature on the transaction slip. In accepting credit cards, even more important is to follow the credit card company's procedures carefully. If the company requires you to get authorization for all credit card sales over $50, then be sure to get that authorization. This may seem time-consuming and troublesome, but the rules are well-grounded. If you have made a credit card sale without fol-lowing the instructions and the credit card turns out to have been stolen or otherwise invalid or the buyer has exceeded his or her credit limit, you are likely to be stuck with the loss.

Further, a buyer who is dissatisfied with the sale for legal reasons, such as breach of warranty, may be able to challenge the charge and the credit card company will "charge back" any payment made to the seller. Craftspeople, therefore, take some ongoing risk when credit card trans-actions are involved.

Personal Checks

The most common difficulty occurs when personal checks are used in payment. A host of things can prevent a check from being honored or cashed by a bank.

To begin with, the person who writes the check may be an impostor, using a checkbook that actually belongs to someone else. In order to reduce the likelihood of this occurrence, craftspeople should insist upon seeing at least two pieces of identification, one of which must contain a photograph of the person, and both of which, ideally, contain information consistent with that printed on the check. Most states' drivers' licenses include a photograph. A current major credit card or a check guarantee card with photo and signature facsimile are also good. Do not accept as identification such items as a Social Security card, a library card, or any ID that can be easily obtained or forged.

Watch while the person signs the check (signatures may have been previously traced from a valid signature) and compare the signature with the signature on the other identification. While only an expert can identify a good forgery, clumsy attempts by amateurs may easily be recognized.

To further protect yourself, accept checks only if they are made out to you and only if they are written for the exact amount of the sale. In other words, do not take third-party checks endorsed to you, never cash a check, and do not take checks for more than the sale amount.

Even if the individual writing the check is legitimate, other possible problems still may exist. One of the most common difficulties is the problem of insufficient funds to cover the check. If the amount of your sale is substantial, it would be prudent to request a certified or bank-guaranteed check. This, however, may deter impulse purchases and is thus not practical for most craftspeople and crafts retailers.

If the person writing the check is known to the recipient, the risk of having a check bounce is minimal. If, however, the crafts sale is to a stranger, the risk of receiving a bad check and not being able to locate the buyer afterward can be reduced if the purchaser's address and phone number are copied onto the check from the supporting pieces of identification (if they are different from those printed on the check). One should also be wary of an individual presenting a check from a bank outside the local area, vacationers notwithstanding.

Despite all these precautions, some bad checks do slip through. A check returned for insufficient funds can be redeposited in the hope that the check will be covered the second time through (most banks will permit a check to be redeposited once). Some bad checks are simply the result of a miscalculation or of the buyer having received a bad check. It is always a good idea to make a phone call before filing a lawsuit.

In most states, it is a crime to obtain property by using a bad check. While you can sue to recover the amount of the check, even if the check-writer cannot be found, any judgment will be effectively worthless unless it can be satisfied. If you win the suit, most states will allow the recovery of reasonable costs of litigation, including reasonable attorney fees. Litigating a claim in small claims court (which may, as a practical matter, be cost-effective for small amounts), will not entitle you to recover your attorney fees.

PAYMENT AFTER WORK IS SOLD OR AFTER AN INVOICE IS SUBMITTED

If you sell through a dealer, there are at least two possible arrangements. First, the craftswork may be consigned, and payment is due only after the work is actually sold. Unfortunately, it is not uncommon for a dealer to neglect to inform a craftsperson of a sale or to delay notification for an unreasonably long period of time. In addition, in recent years, many retail outlets were forced into bankruptcy, thus subjecting the craftsperson to the possible loss of works. (For more detailed information, refer to chapter 4, which deals with the legal ramifications of consignment selling and contains suggestions for protective steps that can be taken under the Uniform Commercial Code, especially in states where specific consignment protection legislation does not exist.)

The other method of doing business is for the craftsperson to be paid after submitting an invoice to a wholesale buyer. Commonly, invoices are payable within a specified time, usually thirty days after they have been tendered. Unfortunately, this system virtually guarantees that the craftsperson will not receive payment until the invoice is due. Indeed, unless some inducement for early payment is offered, the craftsperson may wait interminably to be paid.

Cash Discounts

A simple way to encourage early payment of invoices is to offer cash discounts. The offer of a 5 percent cash discount for early or even on-time payment may be all the encouragement some purchasers need. If the dealer is earning more interest on his cash reserves than is offered as a discount, however, the cash discount will have little appeal.

Charging Interest on Overdue Payments: Pros and Cons

The other option, which can be combined with the incentive of cash discounts, is to charge interest on payments past the invoice due date. This method contains two possible traps. First, many states still have usury laws that limit the percent of interest that can be charged. A lender who exceeds the legal interest ceiling may find that the entire debt is forfeited, all interest is forfeited, or that a usury penalty is imposed.

The second possible problem is the necessity to comply with the federal Truth-in-Lending Act and the various equivalent state laws. On the face of it, a law called Truth-in-Lending would not seem to be applicable to a craftsperson selling works, but the law applies to most transactions in which interest or a finance charge is imposed. The Truth-in-Lending Act is basically a disclosure law, requiring that certain terms be included on any contract or billing that charges interest. The disclosures have been simplified and the task of compliance is further eased by the availability of preprinted forms that contain the required disclosures. While many of the required terms may seem to be inapplicable to a simple sales transaction, if you want to charge interest, then you would be well-advised to use a form that contains all the disclosures. These forms are available from legal publishers and may be tailored to your business by a business attorney.

IF THE PAYMENT NEVER COMES . . .

If neither the carrot nor the stick is effective in obtaining payment, you have several methods by which to proceed.

The first option is to do nothing. If the amount is small enough, you may simply decide not to pursue collection. Needless to say, if this alternative is selected, you should refrain from doing any future business with that customer. You may also wish to write a letter demanding payment. For a sample collection letter, see appendix E.

A second option might be to hire a collection agency to attempt to collect the debt. Collection agencies generally charge a commission of 10 to 15 percent of the recovered amount, although some agencies require an up-front fee and take a lower percentage, and still others charge a fixed fee. Many collection agencies, however, do not accept single-transaction accounts.

LAWSUIT

A third option is the instigation of a full-scale lawsuit to force payment. Under the rules in many states, a formal demand for payment must be made prior to commencing a lawsuit. This option is practical only if the outstanding debt is relatively large. An attorney must be hired and will likely be quite expensive, particularly if the case proceeds to trial.

Also, the court fees charged for filing a case are significant, and the debtor must be personally served with notice of the suit. This is most often done by hiring a process server, another expensive proposition, assuming the debtor can be located. Lastly, even if the case is won, if the buyer still refuses to pay, further proceedings must be initiated to enforce payment. All in all, the expense involved in a civil trial may amount to more than the debt itself. You should discuss the options with your attorney before deciding how to proceed.

Small Claims Court

A simpler and less expensive option is to bring an action in small claims court. While the rules vary from state to state, all of the systems are geared toward making the process as swift, accessible, and inexpensive as possible. Moreover, most courts have staff members who help guide people through pleading and practice in small claims court.

The major savings in a small claims court proceeding are that the filing fees are comparatively low, and the fact that attorneys are not customarily permitted in such courts. Unless they represent themselves or a business entity, attorneys are not generally allowed to assist with completion of the necessary forms or to appear in court. Even in states where attorneys are not specifically barred by statute, the court rules are set up in such a clear, comprehensible way that an attorney is usually not needed.

A small claims suit has some other advantages over a conventional lawsuit. Not all actions, however, can be brought in small claims court. As the name implies, only claims for small amounts can be brought. The definition of "small" ranges from up to $500 in Arizona to up to $5,000 in Oregon. Moreover, only suits for monetary damages are appropriate for small claims court. Other forms of relief, such as an injunction or specific performance, are not available.

Once initiated, the small claims court process is relatively swift and inexpensive. Filing fees are generally under $50. In addition, in most courts, the creditor is not responsible for informing the debtor that a suit has been brought; the clerk of the court customarily mails the notice to the defendant.

In many states, hearings on small claims actions may be held on weekends or evenings. The procedure in the hearing itself is meant to be quite simple. The technical rules of evidence and of legal procedure are generally not followed. The judge simply hears both sides of the case and allows the testimony of any witnesses or evidence either party has to offer. This is truly intended to be a "people's court." Jury trials are never permitted in small claims court, although the defendant may be able to have the case moved to a conventional court if he or she desires a trial by jury.

An action in small claims court also, however, has certain disadvantages. First, the judgment is often absolutely binding: neither party may appeal. Where appeal is allowed, as in New York State, the party wishing to challenge the judgment must show that a grave injustice has been done. This is not easy.

The other major disadvantage of a small claims action is that the judgment may be uncollectible. In many states, the usual methods of enforcing a judgment—garnishment of wages or liens against property— are unavailable to the holder of a judgment from small claims court. In other states, such as New York, enforcement action can be taken only if the debt involved is the result of a business transaction and the debtor has at least three other outstanding small claims court judgments.

For the most part, careful screening of customers will minimize the need to use legal means to collect payment for sales. However, if all other methods fail, small claims court is by far the least expensive and easiest way to obtain legal redress for an outstanding debt. It does, nevertheless, have some drawbacks that should be considered before you decide to use it as a remedy.

PROBLEMS WITH PAYMENTS FROM GALLERIES

Most craftspeople do not operate their own retail shops. Rather, they market their work through other outlets, such as stores and galleries. With gallery owners, it is common practice to take a work on consignment and pay for it after it has been sold.

As discussed in chapter 4, craftspeople should always use contracts when consigning work, specifying what has been consigned, what the financial arrangement is, when the work is to be paid for, how long it is to remain on consignment, who is responsible for insurance, and so forth. Many states now have laws regulating the relationship between creative people and the galleries with which they deal.

Gallery Bankruptcy

Some of these laws were enacted as a result of an unfortunate scenario that has occurred with alarming regularity in recent years. Artists and craftspeople would consign work to a gallery, expecting to be paid within a reasonable time or to have their work returned in good condition, and would learn sometime later that the gallery had gone bankrupt.

Congress recently enacted significant revisions to the Bankruptcy Code. The effective date for most of the provisions is October 17, 2005. Several provision, including a means test limiting eligibility for bankruptcy protection under Chapter 7 of the Code, modifications to exemptions, and restrictions on discharge, reduce the ability of individuals to file Chapter 7 bankruptcy and discharge their debts. The changes are expected to move more debtors into reorganization, primarily Chapter 13 bankruptcies, with required payments for five years. As discussed more fully below, it is essential that, as creditors, craftspeople file their claims and participate in the bankruptcy case in order to maximize their recovery in a bankruptcy situation.

When a bankruptcy petition is filed, the debtor and his or her lawyer are responsible for filing an accurate list of creditors with the court. The court sends a notice of the filing to the listed creditors and gives additional notices to all parties who are listed with the court or who make an appearance in the case.

Craftspeople who have work on consignment in a gallery are among the creditors if that gallery goes bankrupt, but many craftspeople do nothing when they receive the required notification from the bankruptcy court, and thus they get nothing. It is far wiser to reply to the request for information from the bankruptcy trustee and to appear at any creditors' meetings. Craftspeople could get together and appoint one of their number as the deputy for purposes of appearing at creditors' meetings, or they could pool their resources and hire an attorney for this purpose, especially if the meeting is in another city or state. This will, of course, cost some money. Even if the amount at stake in the bankruptcy is small, and it seems that it may not be economically practical to pursue the matter, you should file a claim if the court gives notice to do so. Many creditors fail to file claims, often increasing the payment to those who do.

Precautions: Consignment Laws

The most prudent way to deal with the possibility of a gallery becoming insolvent is to take some precautions before the event occurs. Many states have special laws dealing with consignments, and those laws set up some form of protection for creative people who consign their works. (See chapter 4 for more information regarding consignment.) Article 9 of the Uniform Commercial Code, which has been adopted in every state, also contains a procedure whereby craftspeople can fill out a form called a UCC-1, file it with the appropriate government office (set forth in the form) in the state where the consigned work is located, and obtain secured protection in the consigned work while it is in the gallery.

It should be noted that every state form is slightly different. Therefore, it is essential to use the form bearing the name of the state in which you are filing. The document must be filed in the state where the business is located (which may not be the state where the gallery is located).

The purpose of filing a UCC-1 is to establish a public record and inform all gallery creditors that the works that appear in its inventory are, in fact, owned by someone other than the gallery. Remember, when you consign work, the work is still your property, even though it is on the gallery's premises waiting to be sold.

If you have filed the proper UCC documents to establish your ownership of the goods and then the gallery to which you have consigned the work goes bankrupt, all your work should be returned to you. If, for some reason, the security interest you have established is for less than the full value of the work, the bankruptcy trustee may sell the items and pay you only the amount of the security interest that your UCC documents indicate.

BANKRUPTCIES

Straight Bankruptcy

There are two general categories of bankruptcy. The first, referred to as *straight bankruptcy* in chapter 7 of the Bankruptcy Law, contemplates the prompt conversion of all of the bankrupt's nonexempt property to cash and the payment of creditors, and is available to both individuals and business entities. The Bankruptcy Law establishes a hierarchy of creditors, giving some creditors priority for payment. Such creditors would be the U.S. government (for taxes) and secured parties (see next section), for the amount of their security interests. Each category of creditor must be paid in full before a lower priority creditor may be paid at all. If there is not sufficient money to satisfy all creditors in a particular class, the members of that group will receive a prorated portion of their claim.

As noted above, not all of the bankrupt's assets are available for creditors. There are some things that may be retained, such as a modest house, a holy book, clothing, and the like, even after bankruptcy. The list of exempt property varies from state to state, though there are federal exemptions, too. In some states, the debtor can choose whether to use the state or federal exemptions. In other states, debtors must use the state exemptions. There are also certain exemptions, such as Social Security, that are not part of the bankruptcy laws but may nevertheless apply.

If no party objects to the debtor's discharge or to the discharge of certain types of debt before the deadline set by the court (usually sixty days after the meeting of creditors), the court will enter an order of discharge preventing creditors from pursuing their claims against the debtor. Certain claims cannot be discharged in bankruptcy. Certain types of claims remain intact with no action on the part of the creditor (such as certain categories of tax debts and clear support obligations). Some claims require the filing of a complaint with the bankruptcy court before the discharge deadline.

Reorganization

The second type of bankruptcy proceeding is the reorganization under Chapter 11 of the Bankruptcy Code, which is available to business entities. It contemplates a somewhat different process. Rather than terminating the business, a reorganization is designed to facilitate an orderly payment to creditors so that the business may survive.

After the Chapter 11 petition is filed and the creditors meet, a reorganization plan is proposed by the debtor, though after a prescribed period of time, any party can propose a plan. Once a plan is prepared, it is presented to the bankruptcy judge. If it is determined that the plan meets the requirements of the Bankruptcy Code and the creditors have had an opportunity to vote on the plan, the court may confirm the plan. This is true in some circumstances even if certain creditors vote no, if the court determines that the plan is fair and equitable and does not discriminate unfairly.

Creditors customarily receive more under a Chapter 11 proceeding than they do under Chapter 7, although reorganization is feasible only when a healthy business is suffering from a temporary economic reversal or extraordinary problem. Creditors who have a secured position, such as those who have filed UCC documents to establish their security interest (discussed above), may participate in drafting the Chapter 11 plan. The plan will be "fair and equitable" insofar as the secured creditors are concerned, and they may be forced to agree if it provides that they do any one of the following:

• Retain their liens and receive future cash payments equal to the value of the security
• Retain a lien on the proceeds from the sale of their collateral
• Receive the equivalent of their interests, such as cash up front or substituted collateral

In a Chapter 11 proceeding, a secured creditor may be forced to take a less favorable position than the Uniform Commercial Code would allow in order to have the plan accepted by all the creditors, but a craftsperson with a security interest is still far better off than one who is unsecured.

CHAPTER 13

Individuals, such as sole proprietors, who satisfy certain criteria, may file for bankruptcy protection under Chapter 13 of the Bankruptcy Code, as an alternative to Chapter 7. A Chapter 13 bankruptcy is similar to Chapter 11, in that a plan is worked out between the bankrupt and its creditors for timely repayment of all or a portion of the individual's obligations. Chapter 13 plans generally run for 36 months, and typically require the debtor to make regular payments to the Trustee for disbursement to the creditors on a prorata basis.

Common sense, diligence, and attention to detail are always important attributes for any businessperson. When the economy is weak and money is tight, they become essential. There will probably always be some deadbeats and some uncollectible bills, but with proper care and some preventative maintenance, you can keep these to a minimum.

KEEPING TAXES LOW

A lthough artists and craftspeople rarely think of themselves as being involved in the world of commerce, the IRS treats the professional craftperson like anyone else in business. Thus, the craftsperson has many of the same tax concerns as any other businessperson. In addition, most craftspeople have some special tax problems.

First, the professional craftsperson generally does not work for a fixed wage or salary. As a result, income can fluctuate radically from one tax year to the next. Second, many tax rules designed to facilitate investment may not be useful to the craftsperson. Craftspeople can, however, benefit from certain provisions of the Internal Revenue Code to reduce their tax liability. In this chapter I will cover income-tax issues only. Since sales tax is applied by local authorities and varies from place to place, you should consult with your business lawyer or tax advisor with respect to specific details about this form of taxation.

RECORDKEEPING

In order to take advantage of all the tax laws that are favorable to you, it is imperative that you keep good business records. The Internal Revenue Service does not require that you keep any particular type of records. It will be satisfied so long as your recordkeeping clearly reflects your income and is consistent over time so that accurate comparisons from year to year can be made when evaluating your income. For a sample form that may be used for some relevant tax-related data including bartering, see appendix D(1).

The first step to keeping business records that will allow you to maximize your deductions is to open a business checking account. Try to pay all your business expenses through this account. If using a check, be sure to fill in the amount, date, and reason for each check on the stub. If the check was written for an expense related to a particular client or job, be sure to put the client's name or a job number on both the check and the stub. If your bank allows, keep all of your canceled checks. For expenses paid for with the accounts debit card feature, you should keep the same information outlined above on the actual receipt. For any expenses that you may pay for out of our own personal funds, you should fill out an expense reimbursement form and attach all receipts to this form and write yourself a check out of the business bank account for reimbursement of these expenses.

Second, you should file for a taxpayer identification number. Depending on your circumstances, this may include federal, state, and local identification numbers. In most states and in some cities, the sale of craftwork is considered a business subject to sales tax. You will need to contact your state and city sales tax bureaus to find out their requirements. Usually, a bureau will issue you a taxpayer identification number after you fill out some forms. Then you, as a manufacturer, can buy certain equipment and supplies without paying the sales tax. However, you will later have to act as an agent of the state, collecting sales tax from your customers and paying it to the state. Be aware that even if you do not collect the sales tax from your customers, you will be liable for paying it.

Third, keep an expense diary, which is similar in form to a date book. Use this expense diary on a daily basis, noting all cash outlays, such as business-related cab fares, tolls, tips, and emergency supplies, as they occur. This will satisfy the IRS requirement that, for expenses over $75, you have both a receipt and good evidence of the business purpose of the expense listed in a logical way (such as in a diary). You should also keep an auto mileage log in this diary for all business miles.

INCOME TAXES

There are two principal ways of reducing tax liability. First, craftspeople can spread their taxable income (and thus reduce tax liability) by using several provisions in the tax code. Second, there are significant tax deductions that are available to craftspeople.

One strategy for craftworkers in high tax brackets is to divert some of their income directly to members of their immediate family who are in lower tax brackets by hiring them as employees. Putting dependent children on the payroll can result in tax savings for professional craftspeople who are in a higher tax bracket, because they can deduct the salaries as a business expense. Also, if the business is unincorporated, then no Social Security and Medicare taxes have to be paid in connection with these wages. This salary arrangement is permissible so long as the child is under eighteen years of age. In addition, your child can earn up to the amount of the standard deduction without having any tax liability. The standard deduction (filing singly) for 2004 is $4,850, with adjustment for inflation in subsequent years.

There are some restrictions on placing children on the payroll:

1. The salary must be reasonable in relation to the child's age and work performed
2. The work must be necessary to the business
3. The child must actually do the work

The Internal Revenue Code does not allow a child to claim a personal exemption if he or she is claimed on the parent(s) return, e.g., when the child is a full-time student for whom the parent provides more than half of his or her support.

A second method of transferring income to family members is to create a family partnership. Each partner is entitled to receive an equal share of the overall income unless the partnership agreement provides otherwise. The income is taxed once as individual income to each partner. Thus, the craftsperson with a family partnership can break up and divert income to the family members, where it will be taxed according to their respective tax brackets. The revision in the tax law, as of this writing, created six graduated tax rates for individuals: 10 and 15 percent on the lowest taxable income range, 25 and 28 percent on income in the middle taxable ranges, and 33 and 35 percent on income in the highest taxable income ranges. Capital gains taxes for most investments held at least twelve months were cut from 20 percent to 10 and 15 percent by the 2003 tax law changes. This creates a chance for considerable savings. The income received by children may be taxed at significantly lower rates, resulting in more income reaching the family than if it had all been received solely by the craftsperson, who would be, presumably, in a higher tax bracket than the children. The law stipulates, however, that if a child is under fourteen years of age and receives unearned income from the partnership, any amount over $1,500 will be taxed at the parent's highest marginal rate.

Although the IRS allows family partnerships, it may subject them to close scrutiny to ensure that the partnership is not a sham. Persons designated as partners must have control consistent with that status. In the case of a minor, that control can be exercised by a fiduciary, or the minor can be a limited partner.

Unless the partnership capital is a substantial income-producing factor and partners are reasonably compensated for services performed on the partnership's behalf, the IRS may forbid the shift in income by relying on the UCC section that deals with distribution of partners' shares and family partnerships. This section also provides that a person owning a capital interest in a family partnership will be considered a partner for tax purposes, even if he or she received the capital interest as a gift. Such a gift must be genuine and irrevocable.

INCORPORATING A FAMILY

Some families incorporate in order to take advantage of the potentially more favorable tax treatment. If the IRS questions the motivation for such incorporation, the courts will examine the intent of the family members. If the sole purpose of incorporating was tax avoidance, the scheme will be disallowed.

The various tax reforms have reduced the individual income tax rates so that, for most taxpayers, the rates are substantially in line with or lower than the tax imposed on corporations. The problem of double taxation on dividends, as explained in chapter 1, also exists. It seems, therefore, less advantageous to incorporate. However, one advantage of incorporating is that you can obtain the limited liability advantages discussed in chapter 1.

The benefits of C incorporation have diminished in recent years as 100 percent of health insurance premiums are now allowed as a deduction by individuals as well as C corporations. In addition, the use of the corporate form of doing business is no longer necessary for setting up a retirement plan. Revisions to the rule for individual retirement accounts (IRAs), Keogh plans, and 401(k) plans now allows a self-employed person to set aside as much money for retirement as could be done through a corporate retirement plan.

A craftsperson may also elect to incorporate and be taxed as an S corporation. This enables the corporation to insulate the craftsperson from personal liability while permitting the business to be taxed as if it were individually owned.

If the craftsperson employs a spouse and children, their salaries are considered business deductions, which will likely reduce the craftsperson's taxable income. When the spouse and children are given shares of stock and made owners of the corporation, all the benefits discussed in the preceding section on partnerships are available. Note, however, that if the losses of the investment are considered "passive" losses for the spouse and children, then these passive losses may be used only to offset earnings from other passive investments and are not deductible against ordinary income. As for the unearned income received from the corporation by a child under fourteen, the same rule applies as in a family partnership; amounts over $1,500 are taxed at the parents' rate.

If the craftsperson, as employee of the S corporation, is paid a nominal salary and significant dividends are declared, this dividend income is not subject to Social Security or withholding taxes. However, the IRS has been known to reclassify these dividends as *constructive wages*, thus making the corporation liable for these taxes. A craftsperson should carefully consider the advantages and disadvantages of forming a family partnership or incorporating in light of his or her specific situation and needs.

There is a further advantage to incorporating, whether as a C or S corporation. The corporation and a shareholder can enter into a contract that obligates the corporation to purchase the shareholder's stock when the shareholder dies. The corporation can then purchase an insurance policy on the life of the shareholder in order to provide funds for the stock purchase. The life insurance premiums paid on behalf of an owner, or any person who has a financial interest in the business, are not deductible as a business expense if the business directly or indirectly is the beneficiary of the policy.

LIMITED LIABILITY COMPANIES

As discussed in chapter 1, the limited liability company is the newest business form, and, in general, it provides the same form of liability shield as a corporation. It was also pointed out in chapter 1 that this business form may elect to be taxed as if it were a C corporation or as a pass-through, like a sole proprietorship or partnership. The taxation rules discussed for corporations would therefore apply to LLCs, though, as of this writing, the IRS has not permitted LLCs to elect to be taxed directly as S corporations. If an LLC wishes to be treated the same as an S corporation for tax purposes, the LLC must elect entity status and if it qualifies as an S corporation, i.e., no more than 100 owners who are individuals (there is a limited excepted for estates) and there is only one class of voting interest, then the LLC entity may elect S tax status.

BUSINESS DEDUCTIONS

Until now, we have been discussing the ways craftspeople can spread their taxable income. Another means of reducing tax liability involves making use of deductions. Craftspeople may deduct their business expenses and, thereby, significantly reduce taxable income. As with other artists, they must be able to establish that they are engaged in a trade or business, not merely a personal hobby or else the "hobby" rules will come into play with their taxes. If considered a hobby, the hobbyist or dilettante is not entitled to trade or business deductions beyond the income of the hobby.

To help you avoid the hobby rules, you should keep full and accurate records. Receipts are a necessity. Furthermore, it is best to have a separate checking account and a complete set of books for all of the activities of your trade or business.

Tax laws presume that a craftsperson is engaged in a business or trade, as opposed to a hobby, if a net profit results from the activity in question during three out of five consecutive years, ending with the tax year in question. If the craftsworker has not had three profitable years in the last five as a craftsperson, the IRS may contend that he or she is merely indulging in a hobby, in which case a *profit motive* will have to be proven to claim business expenses. Proof of profit motive does not require the person to prove that there was some chance a profit would be made; it requires proof only of intention to make a profit.

The Treasury Regulations call for an objective standard on the profit-motive issue, so statements of the craftsperson as to intent will not suffice as proof. The regulations list nine factors to be used in determining profit motive; however, this list is not all-inclusive:

1. How the taxpayer carries on the activity (i.e., effective business routines and bookkeeping procedures)
2. The expertise of the taxpayer or the taxpayer's advisors (e.g., study in a related area, awards, prior sales or exhibitions, critical recognition, membership in professional organizations)
3. The time and effort spent on the activity (at least several hours a day, preferably on a regular basis)
4. Expectation that business assets will increase in value (a factor of little relevance to the craftsperson)
5. The success of the taxpayer in similar or related activities (past successes, financial or critical, such as good reviews or shows, even if prior to the relevant five-year period)
6. History of the activity's income or losses (such as increases in receipts from year to year, unless losses vastly exceed receipts over a long period of time)

7. The amount of profits, if any, that are earned
8. Financial status (wealth sufficient to support a hobby would weigh against the profit motive)
9. Elements of personal pleasure (if significant travel produces few crafts objects, the court may be suspicious)

No single factor determines whether or not a profit motive exists. The case of *Deering v. Blair* provides an example of how the factors are used. Deering was the executor of the estate of Reginald Vanderbilt, whose financial affairs and residence were in New York. Vanderbilt had purchased a farm near Portsmouth, Rhode Island, because he was interested in horses, and operated it as a business. The business produced little income, but Vanderbilt claimed business expenses of over $25,000 in each of three years.

The court held that, despite the fact that he had several employees and advertised the farm's horse-boarding and rental services, the purpose for operating the farm was not to produce a profit. Rather, the land was used for pleasure, entertaining, exhibition, and social diversion. The fact that Vanderbilt did not rely on the income from the farm for his livelihood was also considered by the court in making its decision. The business deduction was thus disallowed.

In *Engdahl v. Commissioner*, the tax court found a profit motive on the part of the taxpayers who were considering retirement and wanted to supplement their income by operating a horse ranch. The court held that, despite a series of losses, the taxpayers had kept complete and accurate records that were reviewed by an accountant, had advertised the operation, took their horses to shows, and had worked up to fifty-five hours per week on the operation. Additionally, the assets of the ranch had appreciated in value. All of these facts showed that the taxpayers had a profit motive, and therefore, the business-expense deductions were allowed.

Once you have established yourself as engaged in a craft as a business, all your ordinary and necessary expenditures for production are deductible business expenses. This would include equipment and supplies, workspace, office equipment, research or professional books and magazines, travel for business purposes, certain conference fees, agents' commissions, postage, and legal and accounting fees.

Other Professional Expenses
Of the ordinary and necessary expenditures involved in the making of crafts, most are classified as *current expenses*, i.e., items with a useful life of less than one year. Raw materials, such as clay or fiber, small tools,

such as pliers and screwdrivers, and postage are all current expenses, fully deductible in the year incurred.

Some business expenses, however, cannot be fully deducted in the year incurred and must be depreciated. These costs are *capital expenditures*. Professional equipment, such as lathes, saws, pottery wheels, looms, and the like, with useful lives of more than one year, are capital expenditures that cannot be fully deducted in the year of purchase. Instead, the taxpayer must depreciate, or allocate, the cost of the item over its estimated useful life. This is sometimes referred to as *capitalizing* the cost. Although the actual useful life of equipment will vary, the UCC has established fixed periods over which depreciation may be deducted.

The capitalization exemption for freelance authors, photographers, and artists has not been interpreted to apply to craftworkers.

In some cases, it may be difficult to decide whether an expense is a capital expenditure or a current expense. Equipment repair is one example. If you spend $200 servicing a kiln, this may or may not be a capital expenditure. The general test is whether the amount spent restoring the equipment adds to its value or substantially prolongs its useful life. The cost of replacing short-lived parts to keep equipment in efficient working condition does not substantially add to the useful life of the equipment, so that cost would be a current expense and fully deductible. The reconditioning of equipment or repairs in the nature of replacement, on the other hand, significantly extend the equipment's useful life; thus, the costs of these are capital expenditures and must be depreciated.

All of that being said, for most craft businesses, there is an immediate deduction that can be taken when equipment is purchased. This is done through a special election on the tax return in the year of purchase. In 2004, up to $102,000 of such purchases may be "expensed" each year, and need not be depreciated. This is called the "election to expense certain depreciable business assets." In order to take advantage of this provision, you must have a net income of at least the amount of the deduction. Excesses can be carried over to the next tax year.

Commissions paid to sales agents, as well as fees to lawyers or accountants, are generally deductible as current expenses, provided they are incurred as a result of a business transaction or paid to preserve the existing good will of your business or the like. The same is true of salaries paid to assistants and others whose services are necessary for the business. If you hire help, it is a good idea to hire people on an individual project basis as independent contractors rather than regular employees. This avoids your having to pay for Social Security, disability, and withholding tax payments. You must file a form 1099 MISC for independent contractors who earn $600 or more. In addition, you should specify to the worker the job-by-job basis of the assignments, state when each project is to be completed but not the actual hours to be worked, and if possible, allow the person to choose the place where the work will be done (since this emphasizes the person's independence).

Travel, Entertainment, and Conventions

Craftspeople may travel abroad in order to sell work or gather materials and ideas. More common is the craftsworker who might visit another area of the United States.

Although travel solely for educational purposes is not deductible, there may be tax benefits available if trips are business-oriented. For a business trip, whether within the United States or abroad, your ordinary and necessary expenses, including travel and lodging, may be 100 percent deductible if your travel is solely for business purposes, except for "luxury water travel." However, only 50 percent of the costs of business meals and meals consumed while on a business trip is deductible, provided these expenses are directly related to the conduct of business.

If the trip is primarily for business, but part of the time is given to a personal vacation, you must indicate which expenses are for business and which are for pleasure. This is not true in the case of foreign trips if one of the following exceptions applies:

- You had no substantial control over arranging the trip
- The trip was for a week or less
- The nonbusiness activity did not consume 25 percent or more of the total travel time
- A personal vacation was not a major consideration in making the trip

If you are claiming one of these exceptions, be careful to have supporting documentation. If you cannot take advantage of one of these exceptions, then you must allocate expenses for the trip abroad according to the percentage of the trip devoted to business as opposed to vacation.

Though the above rules cover business travel both inside and outside of the United States, the rules for deducting expenses incurred for conventions and conferences held outside of the United States are more stringent. The IRS tends to review more carefully any deductions for attendance at business seminars that also involve a family vacation, whether inside the United States or abroad. In order to deduct the business expense, the taxpayer must be able to document that the reason for attending the meeting was to promote production of income. Normally, for a spouse's expenses to be deductible, the spouse's presence must be required by the craftworker's employer.

In the case of an independent craftsperson who has organized into a partnership, corporation or LLC, it is wise to make the spouse a partner, employee, or member of the board. Often seminars will offer special activities for husbands and wives that will provide the needed documentation later on.

As a general rule, the business deductions are for conventions and seminars held in North America. For conventions held outside of North America, deductions are allowed only if the taxpayer establishes that the convention is directly related to the active conduct of his or her trade or business. A number of factors are relevant including the purpose of the meeting, the activities of the sponsoring organizations, and the places where other meetings have been held in the past.

The IRS looks closely at cruise ship seminars and now requires two detailed statements to be attached to the tax return when such seminars are involved. One statement should substantiate the number of days on the ship, the number of hours per day spent on business, and the activities in the program. A second statement must come from the sponsor of the convention verifying the first statement. In addition, the ship must be registered in the United States, and all ports of call must be located in the United States or its possessions. The deduction is also limited to $2,000 per individual per year. Again, the key for the taxpayer taking this sort of deduction is to be sure to provide careful documentation and substantiation.

Whether inside or outside the United States, the definition of a "business day" can be very helpful in determining whether a trip is deductible. Travel days, including the day of departure and the day of return, count as business days if business activities occurred on such days. If travel is outside the United States, the same rules apply if the trip is for more than seven days. *Any day the taxpayer uses for business counts as a business day even if only part of the day is spent on business.* A day in which business is canceled through no fault of the taxpayer counts as a business day. Saturdays, Sundays, and holidays count as business days even though no business is conducted, provided business is conducted on the Friday before and the Monday after the weekend or on the days on either side of the holiday.

Entertainment expenses incurred for developing an existing business are deductible in the amount of 50 percent of the actual cost. These expenses must have a proximate relationship to the trade or business and be of the type reasonably expected to benefit the trade or business. You must be especially careful about recording entertainment expenses. You should record in your logbook the amount, date, place, type of entertainment, business purpose, substance of the discussion, participants in the discussion, and the business relationship of the parties you entertained. Remember to keep receipts for any expenses over $75.

You should also keep in mind the stipulation in the tax code that disallows deductions for expenses which are "lavish or extravagant under the circumstances," even though no guidelines have been developed to define "lavish or extravagant." If tickets to a sporting, cultural, or other event are purchased, only the face value of the ticket is deductible. If a sky box or other luxury box seat is purchased or leased and is used for business entertaining, the maximum deduction now allowed is 50 percent of the cost of a nonluxury box seat.

A logbook or expense diary is the best line of defense with respect to business expenses incurred while traveling. When on the road, keep the following things in mind:

With respect to *travel* expenses:
- Keep proof of costs
- Record the time of departure
- Record the number of days spent on business
- List the places visited
- Note the business purposes of your activities

With respect to *transportation* costs:
- Keep copies of all receipts in excess of $75
- Keep track of all mileage if traveling by car
- Log all other expenses in your logbook

Similarly, with meals, tips, and lodging, keep receipts for all items over $75. Be sure to record less expensive items in your logbook.

Craftspeople may also take tax deductions for attendance at workshops, seminars, retreats, and the like, provided they carefully document the business nature of the trip. Educational expenses are deductible if the program is meant to maintain or improve current skills; however, care must be taken for the costs incurred to acquire significant new skills, or the educational requirements for a new trade or business.

Craftmakers are also able to deduct dues paid to trade associations; however, if a substantial amount of the money goes toward lobbying efforts or other legislative activities of the association, the deductible amount of the dues is limited to that portion which does not support such activities.

HEALTH INSURANCE

Self-employed persons may deduct 100 percent of the amount paid for medical insurance for themselves, their spouses, and their dependents.

CHARITABLE DONATIONS

The law regarding charitable deductions of a craftsperson's work is not very advantageous. Individuals who donate items they have created may deduct only the cost of materials used to create those works. This provision has had unfortunate effects on libraries and museums, which, since the law's passage in 1969, have experienced enormous decreases in charitable contributions from authors, artists, and craftspeople. The Museum of Modern Art, for example, received fifty-two paintings and sculptures from artists from 1967 to 1969; between 1972 and 1975, only one work was donated. Since 1975, donations have increased but they have not yet reached the pre-1969 level.

Art and crafts dealers, on the other hand, are allowed to deduct the amount paid for the donated object. Collectors can, generally, deduct the fair market value of the piece determined at the time of the donation.

There is, however, one exception to the general rule for collectors and that is the "alternative minimum tax" (AMT). Congress has attempted to close loopholes in the tax system while continuing to encourage certain income-producing practices. The AMT, strengthened in 1986, requires that all taxpayers pay a minimum tax percentage even though a taxpayer's income may come from those practices that Congress wishes to encourage. Under this system, the income base is broadened to encompass income from these preferential practices; however, a lower rate is then applied to the income base. Prior law allowed the unrealized appreciation on donated property to be excluded from the income base. The 1986 law adds this unrealized amount back into the income base, thereby giving the collector a deduction of the price paid for the donated piece.

Current tax law puts a further barrier in the way of charitable donations by requiring that a deduction may be taken only by those who itemize. The previous law allowed a charitable deduction whether the taxpayer itemized or simply took the standard deduction.

Although several modifications of the law have been proposed, Congress continues to resist change in the area of tax treatment regarding individuals' donations of their own work. Some states, however, have been more responsive. Oregon and Arkansas now allow creators to deduct the fair market value of their works donated to qualified charities, provided certain criteria are met, and California treats creative property as a capital asset.

GRANTS, PRIZES, AND AWARDS

Craftspeople who receive income from grants or fellowships should be aware that this income can be excluded from gross income and thus may represent considerable tax savings. To qualify for this exclusion, the grant must be for the purpose of furthering the craftsperson's education and training. If the grant is given as compensation for services or is primarily for the benefit of the grant-giving organization, it cannot be excluded. If, however, all degree candidates are required to perform certain services as a condition of receiving the degree, the grant is not considered partial payment for services and is excluded from income. Amounts received under a grant or fellowship that are specifically designated to cover expenses related to the grant are no longer fully deductible.

For scholarships and fellowships granted after August 16, 1986, the above deductions are allowed only if the recipient is a degree candidate; and the amount of the exclusion from income is limited to amounts used for tuition, fees, books, supplies, and equipment. Amounts designated for room, board, and other incidental expenses are considered income. No exclusions from income are allowed for recipients who are not degree candidates.

The above rules apply to income from grants and fellowships. Unfortunately, the Tax Reform Act of 1986 also put tighter restrictions on money, goods, or services received as prizes or awards. Previously, some awards were excluded from income in certain cases where the recipient was rewarded for past achievements and had not applied for the award. Under the Tax Reform Act of 1986, any prizes or awards for religious, charitable, scientific, or artistic achievements are included in the recipient's income unless the prize is assigned to charity, and the recipient is not required to render substantial future services as a condition of receiving the award. The recipient must also have been selected without having taken any action to receive the prize.

In conclusion, even though many craftspeople do not consider themselves businesspersons, they may be taxed as such. Because many of the tax provisions designed to encourage the investment end of business are not available to craftspeople, you will need to concentrate on other methods of reducing taxes. The methods discussed here—income spreading and taking advantage of a variety of deductions—provide a starting point for reducing taxes. Be careful to avoid going beyond the realm of acceptable tax planning. If a particular deduction is questionable, consult with a competent CPA or tax advisor before taking it. In any case, consultation with competent tax professionals is always advisable to ensure maximum benefits.

7 INSURANCE

Today's insurance business originated in a London coffeehouse called Lloyd's sometime in the late seventeenth century. Lloyd's was a popular gathering place for seamen and merchants engaged in foreign trade. As Shakespeare pointed out in *The Merchant of Venice*, great profit can come from a successful sea voyage, but financial disaster can follow just as surely from a loss of ships at sea. From past experience, these merchants knew that despite their greatest precautions, such disaster could strike any one of them.

Through their dealings in Italy, the merchants had become familiar with the notion of insurance, but there was no organized insurance company in England at that time. So, when these merchants were together at Lloyd's, it became a custom to arrange for mutual insurance contracts. The method employed was for a ship's owner, before the ship embarked, to pass around a slip of paper that described the ship, its captain and crew, its destination, and the nature of the cargo. Those merchants who wished to be insurers of that particular ship would initial this slip and indicate the extent to which they could be held liable. This slip was circulated until the entire value of the ship and cargo was covered. This method of creating insurance contracts was called "underwriting."

Today, the term *underwriting* is used to describe the formation of any insurance contract regardless of the means employed in establishing it. Lloyd's of London still uses a method similar to the one that originated in the coffeehouse, but most other insurance companies secure against loss out of their own financial holdings.

The risks covered by insurance have changed also. The original Lloyd's dealt in maritime insurance only. Now, almost anything can be insured—from a pianist's hands to a Chihuly glass sculpture.

WHY DO CRAFTSPEOPLE NEED INSURANCE?

Although the business of a craftsperson may not be as perilous as that of the seventeenth-century merchant seaman, it is not without risks. Some of the more significant risks include:

- Recent crime statistics show that, even in rural areas, the craftsperson may be subject to burglary. Various methods may be employed to protect against burglary, but none is foolproof.
- The forces of nature—flood, earthquake, some types of fire—are undiscriminating in their choice of victims. You may already have homeowner's insurance against these risks but you may find that your policy is inadequate to cover your craftsworks and materials. Or, your homeowner's insurance may, in fact, not cover these at all (as discussed later in this chapter).
- Selling your work imposes upon you virtually unlimited liability in regard to anyone who may be injured by one of your objects, regardless of how careful you may have been in creating it. The potential magnitude of what this could cost you easily makes even the slightest chance of its occurrence a significant risk. (See chapter 8, Product Liability.)
- Loss of earnings due to illness or accident is a risk common to all craftsmakers. Some craftspeople who rely on one or more partners may suffer a loss of earnings because of a loss of partners or employees through sickness or accident. This risk is far too often overlooked.

All these risks can be insured against through any number of insurance companies. It should be noted, however, that there are some things that you *cannot* insure against. Insurance is similar to gambling in that it involves an outlay of some money and, if a certain event occurs, you get back many times more. If the event does not happen, you get back nothing. But that is where the similarity ends.

Public policy will not permit you to insure something unless you have an *insurable* interest in it. To have an insurable interest, you must have a property right, a contract right, or a potential liability that creates a real expectation of loss to you if a given event occurs. The rationale behind this is simply to minimize the temptation to cause the calamity against which you are insured. History contains many gruesome stories of desperate or insane people obtaining insurance on, say, a neighbor's barn or even on a neighbor's child.

Of course, the requirement of an insurable interest has never stopped anyone from hastening that interest's demise or destruction. Recently, two businessmen were overheard at a party. One told the other that he had recovered one million dollars in fire insurance that year. The other businessman said he recovered two million for losses caused by a windstorm. The first, with greed in his eyes, asked, "How do you start a windstorm?"

THE BASICS OF INSURANCE LAW

Before analyzing the mechanics of choosing whether to insure a particular risk, a brief outline of the law of insurance may be helpful.

All insurance is based on a contract between the insurer and the insured, whereby the insurer assumes a specified risk for a fee (the *premium*). The insurance contract must contain at least the following:

- A definition of whatever is to be insured (the subject matter)
- The nature of the risks insured against
- The maximum possible recovery
- The duration of the insurance (the term)
- The due date and amount of premiums

When the amount of recovery has been predetermined in the insurance contract, it is called a *valued* policy. An *unvalued* or open insurance policy covers the full current loss of property up to the specified policy limit. The advantages and disadvantages of each will be discussed in this chapter.

The insurance contract does more than merely shift the risk from the insured to the insurance carrier. The insurance industry is regulated by state law. The theory of insurance is to spread a risk among all those subject to that same risk. This risk spreading is accomplished by defining the method used for determining the amount of the premium to be paid by the insured. First, the insurance company obtains data on the actual loss sustained by a defined class within a given period of time. State law regulates just how the company may define the class. An insurance company may not, for example, separate white homeowners and nonwhite homeowners into different classes, but it may separate drivers with many accidents from drivers with few.

The company then divides the risk equally among the members of the class and adds a fee for administrative costs and profits. This amount is regulated from state to state. Finally, the premium is set for each individual in proportion to the likelihood that a loss will occur to him or her. Besides the method of determining premiums, state insurance laws usually specify the training necessary for agents and brokers, the maximum amount of commission payable to them, and the kinds of investments the insurance company may make with the premiums.

The very documents that a company uses to make insurance contracts are likewise state-regulated. States require a standard form from which the company may not deviate, especially for fire insurance. Most states also stipulate that plain English must be used in all forms. "Plain English" is an indexed measure of readability in reference to the average number of syllables per word and the average number of words per sentence. Because of the ruling that insurance contracts are fraudulent if they exceed certain maximum averages, the insurance companies have been forced to write contracts that an average consumer can understand.

EXPECTATIONS VERSUS REALITY

One frequent result of the gobbledygook in which many insurance policies are written is that the issued policy may differ in some respect from what the agent may have led the policyholder to expect. If, however, you can prove that an agent actually lied, then the agent will be personally liable to you for the amount of promised coverage.

Most often the agent will not lie but will "accidentally" neglect to inform the insured of some detail. For instance, if you want insurance for transporting your craftswork, the agent may sell you a policy that only covers transport in public carriers, when you intended to rent a truck and transport it yourself. In most states, the courts hold that it is the duty of the insured to read the policy before accepting it. If, in the above example, you had neglected to read the clause that limits coverage to a public carrier, you would be out of luck. Failure to read the policy is no excuse.

In other, more progressive states, this doctrine has been considered too harsh. Instead, those states will allow an insured to challenge specific provisions in the policy to the extent that they do not conform to reasonable expectations based upon the promises that the agent made. In the example above, it might be considered reasonable to expect that you would be insured when transporting your own goods. If the agent had not specifically brought this limitation of the policy to your attention, odds are that you would have a good case for having an opportunity to amend the provision or have it removed.

Other states follow a different approach for contract interpretation and attempt to ascertain the intention of the parties. The first step in interpreting an insurance policy is to examine the text and context of the policy as a whole. If, after that examination, two or more conflicting interpretations remain reasonable, the ambiguity is resolved against the insurer. A court in these states will assume that parties to an insurance contract do not create meaningless provisions and will favor the interpretation that lets all provisions of the policy have meaning.

Of course, you should not expect an agent to point out these unexpected variations even in the most liberal state. You should read the policy with the agent. If it is unintelligible, ask the agent to list on a separate sheet in plain English all the important aspects before you accept it. Then, retain that list created by the agent and attach it to your copy of the policy to keep in your files.

REFORMING THE CONTRACT OR POLICY

After the insurance policy has been accepted, its terms can be reformed only to comply with the original agreement from which the issue policy may somehow have deviated.

Example: In a case where a woman inherited a pearl necklace, an appraiser, apparently hoping for a large fee, misled her and told her that the pearls were genuine and, therefore, worth $60,000. Before having them shipped from the estate, she obtained insurance on them in the amount of $60,000 and paid a premium of $2,450. In the description of the subject matter, it was stated that the pearls were genuine. When the pearls were ruined after they arrived at the delivery terminal but before she received them, she tried to collect the $60,000. In the course of the investigation of the accident, it was discovered that the pearls were not genuine but cultured and worth only $61.50. Of course, the insured could not collect $60,000 because no genuine pearls had been lost or damaged. The worst of it was that she could not collect even $61.50, because the policy did not cover cultured pearls. The court emphasized that for reformation of the contract to be granted, there must have been something either included or omitted contrary to the intention of both parties. In this case, neither party ever intended to include cultured pearls, so the court refused to amend or make a contract for the parties covering cultured pearls.

You might think that in this case the insured would get back her premium, because there were never any genuine pearls to insure. She argued this, but lost again. The court reasoned that, had the pearls been lost in transit instead of being later destroyed, the actual value of the pearls would never have come to light. Therefore, the insurance company had indeed assumed the risk of paying out $60,000, and thus was entitled to the premium.

OVERINSURING AND UNDERINSURING

By presenting the case of the pearls, I do not mean to propose that if an insured accidentally overvalues the goods no insurance will be recovered. Had the pearls been genuine, but worth only $20,000, she would have recovered $20,000. Note that overinsurance does not entitle one to a recovery beyond the actual value of the goods insured. This is because one does not have an insurable interest beyond the actual value of an item. Allowing a recovery greater than the value of the goods would be inviting people to gamble with insurance policies.

Since you can, at best, break even with insurance, you might think it would be profitable to underinsure your goods. You could gain by paying lower premiums and lose only in the event that the damage exceeds the policy maximum. This also has been tried and was unsuccessful.

Let us study a case where the insured stated the value of her unscheduled property as $9,950 and obtained insurance on that amount. *Unscheduled property* means that an unvalued insurance policy is obtained on some undetermined collection of goods; for example, all a person's clothes and furniture, which may change from time to time. In this case, a fire occurred, causing at least $9,950 in damage.

The insurance company investigated the claim and determined that the insured owned at least $36,500 in unscheduled property. The company refused to pay on grounds that the insured obtained the insurance fraudulently. The court agreed with the insurance company, stating that the intentional failure to communicate the full value of the unscheduled property rendered the entire contract void. The insured, therefore, could not even collect the policy maximum. At best, all she could hope for was to possibly get her premiums back.

Although at first glance, this decision may seem harsh, its ultimate fairness becomes apparent with a little analysis. The chance of losing $9,950 out of $36,500 is greater than the chance of losing $9,950 out of $9,950, simply because most accidents or thefts do not result in total losses.

Various tests are used by the courts to determine whether an omission or misstatement renders a policy void. In all cases, the omission or misstatement must be intentional or obviously reckless, and it must be *material* to the contract. Materiality is measured with reference to the degree of importance that the insurance company assigns to the omitted or misstated fact. If stating the fact correctly would have significantly affected the conditions or premiums that the company would demand, then the fact is material. In the above case, had the full value of the unscheduled property been stated, the insurer would either have demanded that the property be insured for its full value or that a higher premium be paid for the limited coverage. Thus, the misstatement was clearly material.

UNINTENTIONAL UNDERVALUING

It should be noted that not all undervaluations will be considered material. Many insurance contracts do allow some undervaluation where it is unintentional. This provision is designed to protect the insured from inflation, which causes property to increase in replacement value before the policy's renewal date.

A so-called *co-insurance clause* generally provides that the insured may recover 100 percent of any loss up to the face value of the policy, provided the property is insured for at least 80 percent of its full value.

Example: If a house worth $100,000 were insured for $80,000 and suffered a $79,000 loss from a covered casualty, the insured would recover the full amount of the loss, or $79,000. If the same property were only insured for $50,000, then a formula would be used to determine the amount of recovery. This formula requires you to establish a ratio between the amount of insurance coverage and the total value of the property and multiply the resulting fraction by the loss to get the recovery. Inserting numbers in the above formula, we have:

$$\frac{\$50,000 \ (\text{insurance})}{\$100,000 \ (\text{value of building})} \times \$79,000 \ (\text{loss}) = \$39,500$$

This example points out the importance of carrying insurance on at least 80 percent of the value of your property. Because of inflation rates, it would be wise to reexamine your coverage each year.

All insurance policies are limited to certain defined subject matter and to losses caused to that subject matter by certain defined risks. Once the risks are recognized, it is a simple matter to decide whether or not to insure against them. Correctly defining the subject matter of insurance is, however, tricky business. Mistakes here are not uncommon and can result in any one of us finding ourselves uninsured—like the woman with the pearl necklace.

SCHEDULING PROPERTY

The typical insurance policy will include various exclusions and exemptions. For example, most homeowner and auto insurance policies cover personal property but exclude business property. If a craftsperson keeps certain works at home for personal enjoyment, are they personal or business property? The answer depends on whether the craftsmaker ever sells or publicly displays any of these works. If any are sold or publicly displayed, this may convert the entire holding to business property.

In order to avoid the potentially tragic loss of such property, the crafts-person may "schedule" the pieces that are held for personal enjoyment. *Scheduling* is a form of inventorying, whereby the policyholder submits a list and description of all pieces to be insured with an appraisal of their value. The insurer assumes the risk of loss of all scheduled works without concern as to whether they pertain to business or not. Premiums for insurance on scheduled property is slightly more expensive than that of unscheduled property.

Many questions have occurred over the value of objects stolen, destroyed, or lost. In anticipation of such questions, a craftsmaker should maintain records of sales to establish the market price of goods and an inventory of all goods on hand. If some works are scheduled, their value must be ascertained by an expert in the field. This will not avoid all problems, however, because the insurance company can always contest the scheduled value.

WHEN AND HOW TO INSURE

The most important issues regarding insurance are whether to insure or not, and how to obtain insurance.

Deciding Factors

Three factors should be weighed to determine whether or not to obtain insurance. First, you must set a value on that which is to be insured. Life and health are of the utmost value and should always be insured. Material goods should be valued according to the cost of replacement. If you keep a large inventory of your works or if you own expensive equipment, it probably should be insured. The most elementary way to determine whether the value is sufficiently high to necessitate insurance is to rely on the pain factor: If it would hurt to lose it, insure it.

Second, you must estimate the chances that a given calamity might occur. An insurance broker can tell you what risks are most prevalent in your line of work or in your neighborhood. You should supplement this information with your own personal knowledge, for example, knowing that your workshop is virtually fireproof and only a massive flood would cause any real damage. These objective facts should be weighed in your decision. You should not be guilty of hubris, for as the great tragedians have recounted, to scoff at disaster is to invite it. If the odds are truly slim but some risk still exists, the premium will be correspondingly smaller, in most cases.

The third factor to consider is the cost of the insurance. Bear in mind that premiums for insurance purchased to cover your business is tax deductible. Theoretically, Uncle Sam is paying a percentage of the premium equal to your tax bracket.

Keeping the Cost Down

As already noted, the premiums charged by an insurance company are regulated by law. Nonetheless, it still pays to shop around. Insurance companies can compete by offering different packages of insurance and by hiring competent agents to assist you in your choice.

If there are enough craftsmakers in your area, it may be possible for you to form a co-op insurance fund. To do this, you must estimate the total losses the co-op would sustain in the course of a year. Each member then contributes a pro rata share. The money is put into a segregated bank account to collect interest. If a major claim occurs and the losses are greater than the fund, each member must contribute pro rata to make up the difference. If, at year end, there is a surplus, it can be used to lessen the following year's premiums. This method is cheaper than conventional insurance because it eliminates insurance agents' commissions and whatever you would have paid toward the profit earned by the insurance company. Before you form your co-op, though, you should contact an attorney to determine what regulations exist in your state.

PRODUCT LIABILITY

In November of 1978, a California jury awarded the victim of an automobile accident $120 million after his defectively designed Ford Pinto caught fire and exploded, inflicting serious personal injury. The size of this judgment against the Ford Motor Company staggered the nation.

Unless you happen to own a Pinto, you may be thinking, "What does this have to do with me?" The answer is: If you regularly sell your crafts, you might find yourself in court being sued by a customer for an injury if the customer claims that a piece you created is defective. The same laws that apply to the sale of a car by a corporation like Ford apply to a sale by an individual. In one sense, it seems quite logical and fair that the laws apply equally to all, regardless of size. When we take a closer look at the law, however, we see that it was not designed with the small business in mind.

HISTORY OF THE LIABILITY LAW

To understand the present state of liability law, it might be useful to briefly examine its roots. In 1804, a craftsman named Seixas went to a warehouse to buy some braziletto wood, supposedly a valuable wood. Mr. Woods, the warehouseman, sold Seixas some peachum wood instead, which is virtually worthless. Neither party, apparently, knew the difference between braziletto and peachum.

When Seixas discovered the error, he tried to return the worthless wood in exchange for either braziletto or his money. The warehouseman refused, because he had already given the money to the original owner of the purchased wood. Seixas sued Woods and lost, because, even though Woods had written braziletto on the invoice, he never warranted the wood as such and did not know any more about different kinds of wood than did the buyer.

The result of this case can be amply summed up by the Latin maxim *caveat emptor:* Let the buyer beware. This maxim was repeated time and again in both English and American cases until comparatively recent times, but now the pendulum has swung the other way, and the rule has become *caveat vendor:* Let the seller beware. This change has come about gradually.

One of the harshest rules of early product liability cases was that people injured by defective products could not sue the manufacturers unless they purchased directly from them. This technical requirement was carried down the distribution lines, so that only individuals who dealt with each other could have rights against each other, and consumers could not sue anyone but the retailer with whom they had traded. This doctrine was recognized as harsh and rigid; thus, it was discounted in a number of situations.

Example: The seller, regardless of his position in the chain of distribution, could be sued if he were negligent and the product were *inherently dangerous*. The courts struggled for some time over just what was and what was not inherently dangerous. One early case said a car was not. Supreme Court Justice Benjamin Cardozo, in a landmark decision, disagreed. To him, a product was inherently dangerous if injury to the owner was predictable in cases where the item was defective. Almost anything can be injurious if defective, and so the cases hold today. Where once a car was not deemed inherently dangerous, now negligence suits have been brought for such seemingly innocuous items as a toy top, rubber boots, and a lounge chair.

Cardozo made several other important pronouncements in the field of product liability. He stated, for example, that a manufacturer could be liable for defects in component parts made by another manufacturer if the assembler did not inspect them.

This shift of the burden of responsibility from the buyer to the seller was a natural response to several factors. First, as products became increasingly more complex, it was no longer true that the buyer and seller were equally knowledgeable or ignorant. Second, it was felt that businesses were large enough to bear the immediate losses and could, ultimately, spread the risk over an even broader sector of society. Since the majority of the products on today's market are mass-produced by large manufacturers, the present rule reflects the economic reality of industry.

This is not, however, the economic reality of the crafts market, yet it, too, must learn to cope with these laws in a climate of litigious consumers and generous juries. It is better to learn about these problems while you can still protect yourself than when it is too late.

PRODUCT LIABILITY

In every product liability case, the plaintiff must prove that: (1) some injury occurred to the plaintiff; (2) the injury was caused by some defect in the product; and (3) the defect was present in the product when the defendant had control over it. Once people obtain your product, you will not be able to stop them from injuring themselves, but you can control this third element by making sure that any item that leaves your control does not contain a defect.

There are two kinds of defects: mechanical defects, such as loose screws, faulty component parts, and so on; and design defects, such as instability, flammability, toxicity, tendency to shatter, and the like.

LIABILITY FOR MECHANICAL DEFECTS

The scrupulous attention to detail that is usually characteristic of hand-crafted goods almost precludes the possibility of a mechanical defect. If there is a mechanical defect, it will most likely occur in a component produced by someone else.

Example: A stained glass lamp might contain a faulty electrical circuit that could cause serious injury to a user. Obviously, such a defect would be virtually impossible to detect, but under the current rule of *strict liability* followed by most states, you can be held liable for defects that could not have been discovered or prevented by human skill, knowledge, or foresight. Your only protection in such situations is insurance.

Many defects are detectable before an accident occurs if the right tests are made. As pointed out, the courts have held that manufacturers (corporate or individual) have a duty to inspect and test their goods. Failure to adequately test has been held reason enough to impose large awards of punitive damages on top of the actual damages.

Tests and Records

How much testing is adequate? Sophisticated testing might prove to be too expensive for a craftsperson. My advice is to design the best test you can for whatever you make, even if it is only a good tug here and there, and, most importantly, to keep a record of it. This may serve to prove that you attempted to fulfill your duty to test the product. While this precaution might not protect you from product liability, it may result in reducing, if not eliminating, punitive damage being imposed against you.

It is rare for an injured plaintiff to be able to prove that a defect was present when a product was purchased. The plaintiff frequently must rely on inferences drawn from the accident itself. If the jury is convinced that there is better than a fifty-fifty chance that the defect was there when the product was bought, the plaintiff will probably win, but if you come into court with a record of tests on your product, the odds might shift in your favor.

Besides keeping records of your tests, you should also keep records of your purchases of materials and devise some method of identifying the components in your product. This way, if you are sued for a defect in a component part, you can attempt to pass the liability on to the party really at fault. For example, if a stained glass window collapses because the camming is inferior, you might be able to pass your liability on to the manufacturer of the defective cam.

LIABILITY FOR DESIGN DEFECTS

The second category, design defects, can be further subdivided: those that are and those that are not a violation of a statute. A 1959 case contains a good example of how far a court might go in defining a design defect. A rather obese woman entered a store and sat in a chair of contemporary design that the store had for sale. The back of the chair curved elegantly into the seat, which, in turn, curved down and around to form the base of the chair. It was along these serpentine curves that the overweight customer slid onto the floor. The injury to her pride was aggravated by an injury to her spine. The court held that the shape of the chair was defective and awarded her $25,000 in damages.

In defective-design cases, the courts have usually adhered to a common-sense criterion. If the product conforms to the "state of the art" when it was made, it will usually not be held defective. The state of the art is not the same as industrywide standards. Industrywide standards may be introduced as evidence, but it cannot be assumed that these assure due care. This is because the law will not allow an industry to adopt careless practices in order to save money or time when better, more protective methods are available. State of the art, on the other hand, is the measure of how far technology in the field has advanced, that is, how safe the product could be made to be.

A design may be defective if it does not meet the standards set forth in a statute. No product should be sold for consumer use before a check has been made to see whether it is covered by a consumer-protection law. A violation of these laws may carry criminal sanctions. In some jurisdictions, consumers injured by a product have won their case by merely proving that a statute was violated in the production or sale of the product. The manufacturer would then have the burden of establishing that the injury was not the result of the statutory violation, which would be almost impossible in cases where the law had been enacted to prevent the very type of injury alleged. For example, putting small, lovely fastener beads on infants' toys is in violation of state child-safety laws, and such toys would expose the toymaker to liability if an infant choked on the bead.

FEDERAL LAWS
In addition to state legislation pertaining to liability, there are at least three federal laws that directly affect craftsmakers: the Hazardous Substance Labeling Act, the Flammable Fabrics Act, and the Consumer Product Safety Act.

First, there is the Hazardous Substance Labeling Act, as amended by the Child Protection Act of 1966 and the Child Protection and Toy Safety Act of 1969. These statutes were passed in response to the staggering number of injuries and poisonings each year of children under fifteen. Under this Act, as amended, the Federal Trade Commission (FTC) is empowered to name any potentially dangerous substance a *hazardous substance*. Such substances may not be used in any product that might give a child access to the hazardous substance; that is, no amount of use or abuse by a child should make the product unsafe. Presently banned under this Act, for example, are jaquirty beans used in necklaces, jewelry, and dolls' eyes. For a list of other hazardous substances, you should consult your local office of the FTC. Its Web site is *www.ftc.gov*.

The second statute is the Flammable Fabrics Act. This statute empowers the FTC to establish appropriate standards of flammability for fabrics used in clothing and household products, including children's toys.

Finally, there is the Consumer Product Safety Act, a statute that empowers the FTC to regulate the composition, content, and design of a consumer product. The FTC has, for example, promulgated regulations for the use of architectural glass doors, windows, and walls, and has banned the use of any lead-based surface coating materials (paints). This is a dynamic area, and if there is any doubt, craftsmakers should check with the FTC to determine whether the materials they use in creating craft objects are subject to regulation.

The current law of product liability has held the seller, as well as the producer, of a product liable. If held liable for a defective product, the seller may, in turn, seek reimbursement from the manufacturer for the amount paid in damages. This may involve another expensive lawsuit, and, if the manufacturer is broke, the seller is out of luck.

There are three things that might be done by a seller for protection. First, incorporate or use another business form that offers limited liability. This business method is discussed in detail in chapter 1. The second method of self-protection is to obtain insurance. Third, the manufacturer could disclaim all warranties on the craft being sold and merely grant a limited warranty. For more discussion about disclaimers of warranty, see chapter 3. A prudent craftsperson will use all three methods for controlling potential product liability.

LIABILITY INSURANCE

In general, the cost of liability insurance is affordable for the small business. For a person doing up to $10,000 of business a year, liability insurance may cost as little as $100 annually. Rates will vary from region to region. Craftspeople should consult their insurance brokers or agents to determine the rates in their own particular areas. Each craftsperson must then evaluate this cost against the risks of a lawsuit. You should know that the majority of these suits are settled for or are litigated to judgment in excess of $100,000. You can deduct the cost of this insurance as a business expense for tax purposes. Given these factors, if there is any reasonable expectation that a purchaser of your product could sustain personal injury from it, you should seriously consider obtaining product liability insurance.

The area of product liability has evolved to a point where manufacturers are being held liable for injuries caused by their defective products. The doctrines appear to have evolved with an eye to the large manufacturer of mass-produced items but the rules are applied with the same vigor to the craftsmaker creating a unique piece. It is, therefore, important to be aware of the potential risks involved and to take the necessary precautions.

9 TRADEMARKS

Although modern trademark law is a relatively new development, its historical antecedents date back to medieval England. In those days, certain crafts guilds often required their members to place their individual marks on the products they produced, so that in the event a product proved defective, the guild could trace its origins to a particular craftsperson and impose appropriate sanctions. As such, the use of marks enabled the guild to maintain the integrity of its name. Moreover, merchants would often affix marks to their products for purposes of identification. If the product was stolen or misplaced, the merchant could prove ownership by reason of the mark.

The use of marks for purposes of identification would no doubt have worked quite well in an ideal society where all the citizens led principled and moral lives. But such was not the case. Thus, it is not particularly surprising that unscrupulous merchants quickly realized that there was easy money to be made from the use of another's mark, or one confusingly similar. The shoddy craftsmakers could more readily sell their products by affixing to them the marks belonging to quality craftsworkers.

It was in response to this problem of consumer deception that the first trademark laws were developed in the United States. The emphasis was initially on prevention of one person passing off his or her product as that of another. In contrast, modern American law, both common and statutory, focuses upon whether one mark is sufficiently similar to another to cause confusion in the minds of the buying public. The emphasis has thus shifted from the subjective intent of a dishonest craftsmaker passing off goods as those of another, to the objective determination of consumer confusion.

Despite these changes, the essential purposes of trademarks and trademark laws have changed little since the days of the crafts guilds. As discussed below, trademarks still function primarily as a means of identifying the source of a particular product or service. Moreover, trademark laws are designed to enable the trademark proprietor to develop goodwill for the product, as well as to prevent another party from exploiting that goodwill, regardless of whether that exploitation is intentional or innocent.

NEED FOR A RECOGNIZABLE MARK

What, then, is a trademark? A trademark is any word, name, symbol, device, or any combination thereof, used by a merchant or manufacturer of a product to identify his or her goods and to distinguish them from the products of competitors. A service mark is the same as a trademark, except it identifies and distinguishes the source of a service rather than a product. In this chapter, the term "trademark" will be used to refer to both trademarks and service marks.

A trademark benefits the public by indicating the source of the product and helps guide informed purchasing. Manufacturers benefit by using the trademark as a marketing and advertising tool. The key to obtaining protection for a trademark lies in the notion that the trademark must be distinguishable.

The level of protection for a trademark varies with the distinctiveness of the mark. The most distinctive marks are *fanciful* or *arbitrary*. A fanciful mark is one that has no meaning in the language apart from its use as a trademark. The mark "Kodak" that is used to identify photographic supplies and equipment, for example, is fanciful.

Arbitrary marks differ from fanciful marks in that the words are found in the dictionary. Just as with fanciful marks, however, there is no relationship between the mark and the product it identifies. "Shell," the trademark of the petroleum company, is an arbitrary mark, because, although it is a dictionary-defined word, its meaning bears no resemblance to the products it identifies. Fanciful and arbitrary marks are accorded substantial protection by trademark laws.

Suggestive marks—marks that are somewhat descriptive of the product but also require some imagination in order to make the connection—are also protected by trademark laws. "Skinvisible" is suggestive of a transparent, adhesive, medical tape and thus is a valid and protectable mark.

The level of protection may be less, however, if a mark is *descriptive* because merely descriptive marks are not afforded legal protection. These marks merely describe the general attributes or qualities of a product. For example, the name "Raisin Bran" is merely descriptive of the cereal's ingredients, and might have difficulty gaining trademark status.

Descriptive marks can be protected only if the trademark proprietor can prove that the mark has acquired a *secondary meaning*. A secondary meaning exists when the public no longer connects a trademark word with its dictionary meaning, but rather connects the mark with the product it identifies. For example, the registered trademark "TV Guide" has acquired a secondary meaning as the mark of a specific publication that lists television programs and publishes topical articles about the television industry.

Trademarks that merely identify the product for what it is are *generic* marks. The word "beer" is a generic mark and, as such, is not protected by trademark law. In the *Leathersmiths of London* case, the question was whether the name "Leathersmiths of London" was a protected trademark. The court held that the word "leathersmith" is generic, at least when used to describe someone who is in the business of working with leather, and is, therefore, not entitled to trademark protection.

Trademarks that become generic through usage, such as *Aspirin* and *Thermos*, lose their protection. However, if the mark becomes generic with respect to some but not all goods, the proprietor can petition to have registration canceled only as to those goods. For instance, if the trademark *Aspirin* had also been used on bandages and the mark did not become generic with regard to bandages, the trademark's owner could have petitioned to retain the trademark for bandages.

Some trademarks, even though considered distinctive, are, nevertheless, prohibited by statute or public policy. Thus, obscene or scandalous trademarks are generally denied trademark protection. Similarly, trademarks that are deemed deceptively misdescriptive, such as the mark "Idaho potatoes" to identify potatoes produced somewhere other than Idaho, are also denied protection.

PROTECTING A TRADEMARK

In order to secure common law trademark protection, it is not sufficient to merely adopt a distinctive trademark. The trademark must actually be *used* in commerce. The use requirement is fundamental to trademark law and is necessary for common law protection, as well as federal and state registrations. A trademark is deemed to be used when it has been placed in any manner on the product, its containers or the displays associated with it, or on any of the tags or labels affixed to the product. For service marks, "use" is demonstrated by advertising. Thus, it is not always necessary that the trademark actually be physically affixed to the goods. As long as the trademark is associated with the product at the point of sale in such a way that the product can be readily identified as being derived from a particular source, the trademark may be protected.

To ensure common law trademark protection, however, the trademark proprietor would be well advised to physically affix the trademark to the product itself. In this way, the product is certain to bear the trademark when it is sold.

Merely listing a trademark in a catalog, ordering labels bearing the trademark, using the trademark on invoices, or exhibiting trademarked goods at a trade show may not be sufficient in and of itself to constitute use. Use of a trademark *must* be associated with the point of sale.

TRADEMARK LOSS AND INFRINGEMENT

Use is a prerequisite to common law trademark protection, but some forms of use may result in the loss of a trademark. A number of well-known trademarks, such as *Aspirin*, *Thermos*, and *Escalator*, have been lost as a result of improper usage. Generally, trademark protection is lost as a result of the fact that the mark is used in some capacity other than as an adjective modifying a noun. When a trademark is used as a noun or a verb, it no longer functions to identify the source of the product, but rather becomes the name of the product itself. At that point, the mark becomes generic and is not subject to protection.

Once a trademark has been used and adopted, it falls within the purview of common law trademark protection. Common law protects the trademark proprietor against someone else subsequently using a trademark that is confusingly similar to that of the proprietor.

This raises the question of when trademarks are considered to be "confusingly similar." Generally, trademarks will be confusing if they are similar in sound, appearance, or connotation, particularly if the trademarks are affixed to similar products and/or if products are marketed throughout the same or similar geographic areas. If, on the other hand, two products bearing similar trademarks are not related and/or are marketed in different geographic areas, there may not be any infringement.

Thus, a crafts shop that distributes its products solely in the Northwest could probably adopt and use a trademark in use solely in the state of Maine, although if the trademark is registered, it is protected nationwide. Moreover, the Northwest crafts shop could probably adopt and use a trademark used by a Northwest chainsaw manufacturer. In these situations, there may be no infringement, since it is not likely that the use of the mark by the Northwest crafts shop would confuse the public, since the products are so dissimilar, unless the chainsaw trademark was a "famous mark." This concept will be discussed later in this chapter.

It is not necessary to prove actual confusion, i.e., you do not need consumers who will testify that they were confused by the similar marks. The key is the *likelihood* of confusion. Courts will consider the strength of the marks, the similarity of the marks, the goods involved and the market channels, whether the goods are usually bought on impulse or if consideration goes into the decision to buy, as well as the intent of the alleged infringer.

When a trademark has been infringed, the trademark proprietor may sue the infringing party for monetary damages and/or for an injunction prohibiting the infringing use. Monetary damages are measured by either the plaintiff's losses or the defendant's profits from the use of the infringing mark. The plaintiff must prove that the infringement resulted in actual confusion or deception of consumers in order to show lost profits. If the infringement is found to be willful and deliberate, punitive damages can also be awarded, as well as attorney fees.

Courts can also grant an injunction. Pretrial injunctions are rare. The plaintiff must show that:

1. He or she is likely to be successful in a court case
2. There will be irreparable injury if no injunction is issued
3. This injury outweighs any damage that the defendant might suffer from issuance of the injunction
4. The public interest will not be harmed by granting an injunction

REGISTERING A TRADEMARK

Thus far, the discussion has revolved around the trademark protection afforded by common law. It should be noted, however, that the trademark proprietor may procure greater protection under federal and state statutes.

The federal statute governing trademarks is known as the Lanham Act. It is not the function of the Lanham Act to grant trademark rights (since those are secured by the common law, as discussed above), but rather to provide a central clearinghouse for existing trademarks via registrations.

Prior to a 1988 revision of the Lanham Act, the law required that a trademark be adopted and actually used in commerce before the owner could apply for registration. The mark had to be affixed to a product that was sold, shipped, or otherwise used in interstate commerce. This system for registration was criticized, because it required a large investment of time and money in order to create the mark and the product line, as well as getting the line into the stream of commerce.

The 1988 revision eliminates the "actual use" requirement before one can apply for registration of a mark. To apply for registration, you need only state a "bona fide" intent to use the mark in connection with goods or services in commerce. The application must include a drawing of the mark, as well as the filing fee, which is $325 as of this writing if the application is filed online. If the application is sent by mail, the fee is $375. The U.S. Patent and Trademark Office (PTO) reviews the application and looks for similar marks that are at the application stage or are already registered. Once it determines that everything is in order, the PTO will publish the mark in the *Official Gazette,* and anyone who wishes to object has thirty days in which to do so. If no one objects, or the objections are without merit, the PTO will "allow" the mark and send a Notice of Allowance. The mark is *not* registered at this point. The applicant has six months after receipt of the Notice of Allowance to provide the PTO with an affidavit stating that the mark is in commercial use. At that time, an additional $100 is due.

If an applicant fails to commence using the mark in commerce within the allowable six-month period, it is possible to obtain an extension for another six months. This extension is automatic upon application and payment of the appropriate fee ($150), if submitted before the original six-month period expires. Four additional six-month extensions are also possible but require, in addition to application and fee submission before expiration of the current six-month period, approval by the PTO upon a showing of good cause why such extension should be granted. In no event will the PTO permit the period between the date of allowance and the commencement of use of the mark in commerce to exceed thirty-six months. In making a request for extension, the applicant must include the following: a verified statement of continued "bona fide" intent to use the mark in commerce; specification as to which classification(s) of goods and services the intent continues to apply; and inclusion of the required fee, which is currently $150 per extension per classification of goods or services.

The initial filing of the intent-to-use application is considered to be "constructive use" of the mark. This means that your priority for claiming the mark is measured from the date of application. If another person applies to register the same or a confusingly similar mark after your application is received, he or she will be denied registration. This is true even if the subsequent applicant puts the mark into commercial use prior to your doing so, but after your filing date. In effect, this filing allows you to reserve a mark while you investigate the mark and develop the product.

This intent-to-use registration is a supplement to the "actual use" system and not a replacement for it. Applicants may continue to register their marks based on use, and, in fact, no mark is registered until it has actually been used in commerce.

If you have already used the mark, you must provide the PTO with a drawing, a specimen of the trademark as it is being used in connection with or affixed on goods in commerce, and the appropriate filing fee, along with your application. The review process occurs, and, if no problems are found, the mark is published in the *Official Gazette* along with marks originally filed under the intent-to-use provisions. Marks published in the *Official Gazette* that are not opposed within thirty days of publication will be granted a certificate of registration. Registration entitles you, as trademark proprietor, to certain benefits in addition to those afforded by common law (see next section).

Application forms may be obtained by calling the PTO at (800) 786-9199, or by visiting the PTO's Web site at *www.uspto.gov*.

State trademark statutes generally grant rights similar to those of the Lanham Act (some states grant even greater protection), except that those rights do not extend beyond the borders of the state.

In order to obtain trademark protection under state law, the trademark proprietor must file with the appropriate state agency a trademark application along with documentation similar to that required for federal registration. The number of examples of the mark to be furnished and the registration fees vary from state to state.

BENEFITS OF REGISTERING

Registering your trademark carries a few extra benefits that can make it worth your while. First, registration enables proprietors to use the symbol ® in conjunction with their marks, which may well deter others from using them. Proprietors of marks that have not been registered are prohibited from using the above symbol with their marks. Commonly, ™ for trademark or ℠ for service mark are used in conjunction with an unregistered mark or a state trademark, whether or not registered. These designations have no official status, but they do provide notice to others that the user is claiming a property right in the mark.

Second, registration on the Principal Register is evidence of the validity of the registration, the registrant's ownership of the mark, and the exclusive right to use the mark on identified goods in commerce. Some marks not eligible for registration on the Principal Register may be registered on the Supplemental Register. Marks can be registered on the Supplemental Register but not the Principal Register if they are merely descriptive, deceptively misdescriptive, geographically descriptive or misdescriptive, or a surname.

Finally, a trademark registered on the Principal Register that has been in continuous use for a period of five consecutive years generally becomes "incontestable;" that is, the proprietor may secure rights superior to those of a prior, but unregistered user if the original user does not object to the registrant's use within five years of registration. The registrant must file the appropriate documents with the PTO in order for the mark to become incontestable.

A trademark registration remains in effect for a period of ten years and may be renewed in additional ten-year increments by filing an application for renewal at least six months prior to the expiration of the preceding ten-year term. This is a change from the twenty-year period of prior law. During the first ten-year period, however, proof of continued commercial use must be provided. This proof must be in affidavit form and filed during the sixth year of registration. This allows the Register to be purged of marks not being used.

Obviously, registration can be quite beneficial to a craftsmaker who has invested time, money, and energy in developing a reputation for quality work. Procuring trademark protection on either the state or federal level may require a considerable amount of time and skill. In this regard, an attorney may prove invaluable. An attorney can first determine whether the benefits to be derived from registration justify the expenses. The total costs for trademark registration usually run around $1,500, including filing and attorney fees but not including artist's fees (if any) to have drawings made. An attorney can also research a trademark index to determine if there are any conflicting marks, and, finally, can complete the application and deal with any problems that may occur while it is being processed.

ANTIDILUTION

In 1996, federal trademark law was amended to provide special protection to "famous marks." The statute does not define "famous mark," although case law likely will. Legislative history suggests that a *famous mark* is a mark that has been around for a long time and enjoys extensive notoriety.

In the past, it was possible to appropriate a mark for use on goods or services that do not compete with those of the mark's owner, so long as there was no likelihood of confusion. As a result, it was possible, for example, to call a dog food "Cadillac," intending to suggest that it was the elite form of canine fare, despite the fact that the automobile manufacturer did not have anything to do with the dog food. The likely intent of the dog food company was to suggest that it was the "Cadillac" of dog foods and, thus, the top of the line. This type of use will probably no longer be permitted, since the dog food's use of the mark "Cadillac" would likely be considered to be a dilution of the General Motors trademark. While antidilution statutes had been in effect in several states, they were not universal. The federal statute now provides protection for famous marks. The remedies available for violations of the antidilution statute are comparable to those that are provided for trademark infringements.

Dilution is defined as "the lessening of the capacity of a famous mark to identify and distinguish goods or services, regardless of the presence or absence of (1) competition between the owner of the famous mark and other parties, or (2) likelihood of confusion, mistake or deception."

Although the term "famous" is not defined by the statute, a list of factors to be considered in determining whether or not a mark is famous is set forth in the Lanham Act. These factors are:

- The degree of inherent or acquired distinctiveness of the mark
- The duration and extent of the use of the mark in connection with the goods or services with which the mark is used
- The duration and extent of advertising and publicity of the mark
- The geographical extent of the trading area in which the mark is used
- The channels of trade for the goods or services with which the mark is used
- The degree of recognition of the mark in the trading areas and channels of trade used by the mark's owner and the person against whom the injunction is sought
- The nature and extent of use of the same or similar marks by third parties
- Whether the mark was registered under the Act of March 3, 1881, or February 20, 1905, or on the Principal Register

INTERNATIONAL PROTECTION

A trademark can be registered internationally under two multinational arrangements, the Madrid Accord or the European Community registration. For craftspeople desiring to register their trademarks throughout European Community member countries, a process is available. Unfortunately, this requires the assistance of an attorney in an EC member country to apply for registration of the Community mark. The United States is not a party to the Patent Cooperation Treaty (PCT) and, therefore, the craftsperson must begin the trademark protection process in an EC country.

The United States is a party to the Madrid Protocol, and craftspeople desiring registration of their trademarks in other nations that are parties to this treaty can obtain those registrations through the U.S. PTO with the assistance of their U.S. intellectual property lawyer.

For a list of Madrid member nations, consult *www.uspto.gov*; visit *www.uspto.gov/web/offices/pac/dapp/pctstate.pdf* for a list of PCT members.

Craftsworkers interested in contacting attorneys who specialize in trademark work can consult the yellow pages of the telephone directory or online (look for Patent Attorneys or Trademark Attorneys) or consult their state bar associations for some recommendations. The Volunteer Lawyers for the Arts organizations in various states may also be able to assist with referrals (see appendix A).

COPYRIGHT

Copyright law in the United States has its foundation in the Constitution, which provides in Article I, Section 8, that Congress shall have the power "to promote the progress of science and useful arts, by securing for limited times to authors and inventors the exclusive right to their respective writings and discoveries." The first Congress exercised this power and enacted a copyright law. The legislation was periodically revised by later Congresses until 1909. The 1909 Act was substantially revised in 1976, and again in 1988, when the United States became a signatory nation to the Berne Convention, an international copyright treaty.

Prior to the 1976 revision, unpublished works were protected by a so-called common law copyright and various state laws. Federal protection under the 1909 Act was not triggered until publication of the work. Under the 1909 Act, publication meant an unrestricted public display.

The Copyright Revision Act of 1976 preempted state copyright laws, making claims after January 1, 1978, subject exclusively to federal law. Publication under this revision is defined as the distribution of copies of a work to the public by some method of ownership transfer, such as a sale, or by lease or loan. The 1976 revision became effective on January 1, 1978, but it is not retroactive.

The Berne Convention Implementation Act of 1988 applies to claims arising after March 1, 1989. One of the major changes to U.S. copyright law under the Berne Convention is that, for the first time, the law does not require a copyright notice, although notice should be used when possible.

Because of the fact that the 1909, 1976, and 1988 laws all must be considered, depending on when the work was published, there are, in effect, three sets of laws in the field of copyright. The craftsmaker must be aware of the differences in order to fully benefit from the law.

WHAT IS COPYRIGHT?

There are five exclusive rights included in the "bundle of rights" known as copyright. The first is the right of first publication, which is the right to determine when and where your work will first be displayed to the general public or a substantial number of persons outside of family members and social acquaintances. If you have sold a copyrighted work, however, the buyer now has the right to display that work as he or she sees fit.

Second is the right to control the first sale of a work. The only exception may be in cases where lienholders who were involved in producing or processing the work levy upon it for the satisfaction of unpaid debts.

Third is the right to reproduce the work. The Copyright Act of 1976 allows reproduction of works without the copyright owner's consent in a few limited circumstances (see the discussion on the *fair use doctrine* later in this chapter).

Fourth is the right to prepare derivative works based on the copyrighted work. A derivative work is some form of adaptation or transformation of the original work.

Fifth is the right to publicly perform the copyrighted work (where applicable).

These rights are divisible, meaning that they can be transferred in whole or in part. If you take no special action when you sell a work, you will retain all of the above rights except that, once a copyrighted work is sold, the right to control further sales or displays of that work usually ends.

There is a difference between conveying the copyright in a work, which can only be done through a signed writing, and selling the actual piece. You may, however, explicitly transfer or license a particular right if you wish. In order to do so, the transfer must be in writing, signed by the copyright owner or an authorized agent, and must identify the right(s) to be conveyed. A license can be oral, but an oral license may be terminated at the will of the copyright owner.

The copyright law itself does not provide economic benefits. The law vests intangible rights in the copyright owner that allow the owner to bargain for future economic benefits, such as royalties on reproductions.

WHAT CAN BE COPYRIGHTED?

Copyright protection extends to "original works of authorship fixed in any tangible medium of expression." It does not, however, extend to any "idea, procedure, process, system, method of operation, concept, principle, or discovery." Copyright is protection for the form of expression and not the idea expressed. For example, an idea for a piece of jewelry cannot be copyrighted, but the tangible expression of that idea—a ring, for example—is eligible for copyright protection. Likewise, a useful object cannot be copyrighted in itself, but the nonfunctional, aesthetic aspects of such an object are copyrightable. For example, the pattern on a piece of fabric is copyrightable. The items of clothing that are made from that fabric are not copyrightable, however, since they are considered to be useful items. A woven rug would also not itself be copyrightable, although the pattern could be protected.

The 1909 Act required the work to be both original and creative in order to obtain copyright protection. The creativity prerequisite was expressly dropped from the law in 1976, although there is a presumption that minimal creativity must exist in the creation of the work. The requirement that a work be original does not mean that the work must be unique. Originality means only that the work was not copied from another.

Example: Suppose you create a silver bracelet in a limited edition of twenty. The design on each bracelet is copyrightable, because it is original, although not unique. If, by some miracle of circumstances, another silversmith independently creates a bracelet identical to the ones you have created, his or her bracelet is eligible for copyright protection as well, because it satisfies the originality requirement. If, however, the other artist copied your work, he or she would be an infringer. The infringing work would be denied copyright protection, and the infringer would likely be liable to you for damages.

Cartographers who independently create identical maps of a geographic area are each entitled to copyright protection, because each map is original in its creation. Many cartographers will intentionally include a minor error on a map so that if the identical error appears on another map alleged to be original, there will be obvious evidence that copying has occurred. Thus, in the writing of this book, I have intentionally included nonsubstantive errors to inhibit copyright infringement.

WHO OWNS THE COPYRIGHT?

Generally, the creator of the copyrighted work is the owner of the copyright. There are, however, exceptions to this general rule. Under the

1909 law, copyright ownership passed from the creator to the purchaser of the work, unless the creator explicitly retained ownership. As such, when a potter sold a copyrighted pot, the purchaser received not only the pot, but the copyright in the pot as well. The presumption was that copyright went with the sale of the work.

The Copyright Revision Act of 1976, as amended, reversed the presumption that the sale of a work included the copyright. Today, there must be a written agreement providing for the sale of the copyright. Otherwise, the creator of the work remains the copyright owner. If the potter wishes to transfer the copyright along with the ownership of the pot itself, he or she may do so through a written document. For a form that may be used for this purpose, see appendix C(5a).

Joint Works

In a joint work, each contributor automatically acquires an individual ownership in the entire work. Section 201(a) of the Copyright Act provides, "The authors of a joint work are co-owners of copyright in the work." A *joint work* is defined as "a work prepared by two or more authors with the intention that their contributions be merged into inseparable or interdependent parts of a unitary whole." Thus, whatever profit one co-owner makes from a joint work must be shared equally with the other co-owners, unless they have a written agreement stating otherwise.

The key point is the intent that the parts be absorbed or combined into an integrated unit at the time the work is created. The late Professor Melville Nimmer suggested that, although such an intent must exist at the time the work is created, not at a later date, the authors do not necessarily have to work together, work during the same period, or even know each other. However, the joint works definition does not include the situation where an artist creates a work, such as a piano solo, not intending that the work involve another artist, and later commissions lyrics. If there is no intention to create a unitary or indivisible work, each creator owns the copyright only to his or her individual contribution.

In *Ashton-Tate Corp. v. Ross*, the Ninth Circuit Court of Appeals held that joint authorship was not established by the mere contribution of ideas and guidance for the use interface of a computer spreadsheet, because joint authorship also requires each author to make an independently copyrightable contribution.

Derivative Works

In the case of a *derivative work*, the contributing author owns only his or her own contribution. A derivative work is defined as:

A work based upon one or more preexisting works, such as a translation, musical arrangement, dramatization, fictionalization, motion picture version, sound recording, art reproduction, abridgment, condensation, or any other form in which a work may be recast, transformed, or adapted. A work consisting of editorial revisions, annotations, elaborations, or other modifications which, as a whole, represent an original work of authorship, is a "derivative work."

Thus, any work based completely or substantially upon a preexisting work, if it satisfies the originality requirement and is not itself an infringing work, will be separately copyrightable. The distinction between a derivative work and a joint work lies in the intent of each contributor at the time the contribution is created. If the work is created with the intention that each contribution be merged into inseparable or interdependent parts of a "unitary whole," then the merger creates a joint work. If such intention occurs only after the work has been created, then the merger results in a derivative or collective work.

Collective Works

A *collective work* is defined as "a work, such as a periodical issue, anthology, or encyclopedia, in which a number of contributions, constituting separate and independent works in themselves, are assembled into a collective whole."

The originality involved in a collective work is the collection and assembling of preexisting works, which may themselves be copyrightable, without any internal changes in such material. This assemblage of work is copyrightable.

Works Made for Hire

There is an important exception to the copyright ownership rule in the form of the "work-made-for-hire" doctrine. Under this classification, employers are granted the copyright in works created by their employees if that creation is within the scope of the employee's job. The work-made-for-hire doctrine is based on several premises:

- The work is produced on behalf of the employer and under its direction
- The employee is paid for the work
- The employer, having paid all the costs and bearing all the risks of loss, should reap any gain

A work made for hire is defined as a "(1) work made by an employee within the scope of his or her employment, or (2) a work specifically ordered or commissioned" in certain circumstances. For example, if a silversmith is an employee and creates a piece of jewelry within his or her scope of employment, the copyright belongs to the employer. Similarly, if a silversmith were independent and commissioned to create a specific piece of jewelry, then the copyright in the piece would remain the silversmith's unless it was expressly conveyed in writing to the party commissioning the work and the work fell into the statutory category of works made for hire.

The work-made-for-hire provisions of the 1909 Act have been shown in studies by the Copyright Office to have been a historical misstep in terms of the legislative process. The focus of Congress was on staff-written material prepared by salaried employees for publication by an employer-publisher in composite or encyclopedic works. The copyright studies suggest that the legislators did not realize the breadth of the exception they were creating, since it could be applied to a variety of employment situations, such as full-time crafts teachers.

Impracticality of Shared Copyright

There were some proposals, during the hearings on the 1976 Act, to let the employer acquire the right to an employee's work to the extent needed for regular business purposes, but to allow the employee to own all other rights, as long as the employee did not authorize competing uses. These proposals were not adopted for several reasons: the difficulty of defining which uses of a work were competing, the impracticality of applying the language to situations where the work was a composite of many employees, and a potential user's inability to identify owners for the purpose of negotiations.

Although there are no concrete definitions of *employee* or *scope of employment*, the courts have established guidelines for determining whether a work is one made for hire. One element is the existence of an express contract-for-hire, especially if the creator agrees to work exclusively for the employer. Payment of a regular salary is also an important factor. Some courts have found that the crucial question in determining an employment relationship is whether the alleged employer has the right to direct and supervise the manner in which the other person performs the work.

Even if there is a clear employer-employee relationship, the mere fact that an employee creates a work is not enough to make it a work made for hire. It is only when an employee creates a work *within the scope of his or her employment* that the creation is a work made for hire. As one court said in regard to no less a person than Admiral Hyman Rickover, "No one sells or mortgages all the products of his brain to his employer by the mere fact of employment." Thus, the artistic efforts of an employee not produced within the scope of employment remain the property of the employee.

Special Employee Doctrine

Under previous law, a person, although seemingly an independent crafts-maker, was considered an employee if he or she was subject to the super-vision or control of the person commissioning the work. The craftsmaker was considered a *special employee* in this case, and the copyright belonged to the person who commissioned the work.

In *Community for Creative Non-Violence (CCNV) v. Reid*, the U.S. Supreme Court overruled this doctrine. Reid, the sculptor, agreed to sculpt three figures huddled over a steam grate for a nativity scene depicting the plight of the homeless. CCNV would provide the pedestal and steam grate for the scene. The parties negotiated the price and the materials to be used, and CCNV made recommendations concerning the figures themselves. Copyright ownership was not discussed. A dispute arose after the project had been completed, when the parties each filed for copyright registration. Although the lower court determined that the project fell under the work-made-for-hire doctrine and CCNV owned the copyright, the appellate court reversed this ruling, saying that the sculpture did not fall under one of the enumerated classes of projects outlined in the law as being potentially a work made for hire, and there was no writing as required by the law.

The copyright statute now recognizes a long-standing trade practice that the copyright of certain works created by independent contractors belongs to the creator rather than the employer, unless the parties expressly agree in writing that the piece shall be considered a work made for hire. Thus, a work created by an independent contractor is not a work made for hire unless the parties have signed a written agreement to that effect and the work is specially ordered or commissioned as:

- A contribution to a collective work
- Part of a movie or other audiovisual work
- A translation, supplementary work, or compilation
- An instructional text
- A test or answer material for a test
- An atlas

The Work-Made-for-Hire Doctrine and the Craftsworker/Teacher

Most artists and craftspeople who are employed in educational institutions remain independently active and prolific in their creative fields. For some, creating works of art or crafts is a way to further explore the subject they teach, a way to remain creative. For others, it may be a way of supplementing their salaries. It is important to determine whether the craftsperson owns the rights to designs he or she creates or whether the employer owns the rights. In this section, discussion will focus on whether works created by a craftsperson who is employed at an educational institution are works made for hire and whether the institution owns the copyright.

It is important to determine whether these works are made for hire, not only because of the implications of copyright ownership, but also because ownership affects the term of copyright protection. Under the 1909 law, the holder of a copyright is the only person eligible to renew the copyright. Under current copyright law, the term of copyright for works made for hire is 120 years from creation or ninety-five years from first publication, whichever expires first. In many cases, this will be shorter than the usual term of "life of the author plus seventy years." Also, works made for hire are not subject to the termination provisions of the statute, which allow an artist, craftsmaker, or other author to terminate the assignment of a grant or transfer of rights.

As previously discussed, one of the key elements in a work-made-for-hire situation is whether the employer has the right to supervise or control the person in performing the work. In academic settings, professors write and deliver lectures virtually without administrative control. There is, however, some control, since the courses that a professor is hired to teach determine, within certain bounds, what the subject matter of the course should be. Also, the quality of teaching is reviewed by the administration. Since there are elements of control, and teachers or professors receive regular compensation and have express employment contracts—two other factors that the courts consider—they are probably creating their lectures in the scope of their employment.

It is important to determine the *scope* of the employment situation. Much litigation in the employment area arises out of an employee's creation of a work that relates to the job, but is not a part of his or her specific duties. This is the case, for example, when a teacher creates a work of art or craft in the teacher's particular field, but creation of the work was not expressly required as one of the teacher's duties.

In determining scope of employment, control and supervision are crucial issues. Factors to consider are whether the work was edited by the employer or whether there was any control over content and style of the work. Craftspeople can argue that their school/employer has no such control or supervision.

A second criterion to be considered is whether the work was created at the employer's place of business. It generally cannot be assumed that a teacher will or will not use the facilities of the school to create independent projects. However, it has been held that if a work would not otherwise fall within the scope of employment, the fact that even a portion of the work was done using the employer's facilities and personnel does not necessarily render the work the property of the employer.

A third issue is whether the work was created during normal working hours. This may be an unimportant distinction in regard to teachers or professors, since the concept of nine-to-five working hours often is not applicable. Schools usually do not dictate class-preparation time, and it is sometimes difficult to distinguish between a professor's working hours and leisure time. This criterion might more readily apply to elementary or high school teachers, who, in general, have more regular hours. However, even they are more flexible in the time they work than, for example, a factory worker.

The final criterion for determining whether a work was created within the scope of employment is whether it was produced at the insistence and expense of the employer (i.e., was the employer the motivating factor in producing the work?). The outcome of this test depends on the facts of each case. A weaving instructor who creates a rug while demonstrating to the class an intricate weaving pattern is more likely to have created a work made for hire than if she had created a rug on her own time, using her own loom.

There are some situations in the realm of education in which good arguments can be made that the work was not created within the scope of employment. If, however, the educational institution has any control over the work, or the work is done at the time, place, expense, or insistence of the institution, it is probably a work made for hire, and the institution would then own the copyright in that work.

Creative people in the education sector should take some steps to avoid the injustice of the work-made-for-hire doctrine, because many works created by craftspeople who are also employed by educational institutions might be considered works made for hire.

One possible step would be for you to obtain a transfer of copyright ownership from the school. To be valid, there must be a note or memorandum of the transfer, signed by an agent of the school.

A second option is to vary ownership rights through a written contract between the parties involved. The Copyright Act provides:

> In the case of a work made for hire, the employer or other person for whom the work was prepared is considered the author for purposes of this title, and unless the parties have expressly agreed otherwise in a written instrument signed by them, owns all the rights comprised in the copyright.

Thus, a teacher and the school could include a provision in their contract to negate the presumption that the school owns the copyright. This provision must be definite and precisely state what the rights are that the employee retains.

While the parties may vary the rights that would otherwise be owned by the employer, they cannot vary the employer's status as author of the work. This distinction in the Act was intentional and was made in order to prevent parties from avoiding the legal consequences (other than ownership rights) that arise by reason of the status of a work as one made for hire.

DURATION OF COPYRIGHT

The Constitution allows Congress to extend copyright protection for "limited times." The 1909 Act granted protection for twenty-eight years, with an additional renewal period of another twenty-eight years.

For works created on or after the effective date of the 1976 Act (January 1, 1978), the protection period was initially the life of the author plus fifty years. The Sonny Bono Term Extension Act extended the period of protection for all copyrights then in existence by twenty years. If a work is created jointly, the copyright now expires seventy years after the last author died. In work-made-for-hire situations or when the author is anonymous or uses a pseudonym, the period of protection is 120 years from creation or ninety years from publication, whichever expires first. The same periods of protection are given those works created before January 1, 1978, but not published (or registered) prior to that date. These works do not fit under the 1909 provisions because the 1909 Act protects only published works. Because these works were in tangible form prior to the 1976 Act, they do not automatically fall within the protection of that Act either. The earliest date a copyright can expire under this provision was December 31, 2002. If the work was published by that date, there is an extension of twenty-five years from the date the copyright would have expired under the old law.

No renewals are obtainable under the 1976 Act and copyrighted works governed by the 1909 Act in their original term were automatically granted an extension and the period of protection for those works is ninety-five years after publication.

CREATION

Federal copyright law now protects works once they are fixed in tangible form. There are currently no formal requirements of registration, but in order to bring an infringement suit, the allegedly infringed work must be registered. You can register after the infringement has occurred, provided it is before the lawsuit is filed, but statutory damages and attorney fees will not be available remedies. If you register early, there is the added advantage that the information in the registration is presumed to be true if the registration was within five years of the date the work was created. This is so even if you register prior to publication but publish before the five-year period expires.

NOTICE

Under the 1909 Act, notice was required on published works for the works to be protected. If notice did not appear on the work, it was considered, with few exceptions, to be in the public domain. Notice had to appear on the original and on all copies.

For example, the city of Chicago, in *Letters Edged in Black Press, Inc. v. Chicago*, lost the copyright on Picasso's sculpture, the *Chicago Picasso*, because a maquette of the work was placed on public exhibition at the Art Institute without a copyright notice attached. Photographs of the maquette, also without notice, were distributed to the press. The court ruled that the exhibition of the maquette without notice, as well as the distribution of the photographs, caused the work to fall into the public domain. The notice attached to the completed sculpture was invalid, because this sculpture was, in the court's words, "a mere copy, albeit on a grand scale, of the maquette, a work already in public domain."

The 1976 Revision Act provides protection once the work is in tangible form, whether it has been published or not. However, prior to March 1989, in order to retain copyright protection after publication, notice must have appeared on the work. The copyright in a work is not lost if:

1. Notice was omitted on a relatively small number of copies
2. The work was registered within five years of publication
3. A reasonable effort was made to add notice to all copies distributed in the United States

The copyright will also not be lost if notice is omitted by a third party in violation of an express agreement to distribute copies only with the proper notice.

The 1976 revision would likely change the result in a situation similar to the *Chicago Picasso* case. Any one of the three provisions noted above could have been used to save the copyright under the right circumstances.

The 1988 Implementation Act eliminated the requirement for notice on any works that are published after March 1, 1989, although this change was not retroactive. Works published prior to March 1, 1989, must have had the proper notice at all times prior to March 1, 1989 (unless one of the exceptions noted above applies). There are, however, advantages to continuing to affix notice to works even though it is not required by law. One advantage is that, in a copyright infringement lawsuit, the defense of *innocent infringement* is not available if there is proper notice on the work. Innocent infringement involves someone copying a work believing it to be unprotected. Notice attached to the work eliminates this argument. Also, attaching notice to works is an inexpensive way to deter potential infringers.

Proper notice consists of three elements. The first is the word *Copyright*, the abbreviation *Copr.*, or the symbol ©. Note that the letter C in parentheses is not a legal equivalent. Second is the year of first publication. The name of the copyright owner is the third element of notice. The name should be the author's full name, unless the author is well known by last name only. Thus, an example of an appropriate notice is: © 2005 Leonard D. DuBoff.

International notice requirements differ somewhat from the requirements imposed by the 1976 Act. For countries that are covered by the Buenos Aires Convention, another copyright treaty to which the United States is a party, the words "all rights reserved" must appear. If you plan to sell your works in Central or South America, be sure to investigate any special international notice requirements that may be in effect.

The Berne Convention prohibits signatory nations from requiring that notice be placed on works in order to obtain protection. There are more than eighty countries that participate in this treaty.

The Universal Copyright Convention, the third copyright treaty to which the United States is a party, requires the use of the symbol © as part of the copyright notice for protection under it. Most Western European countries are parties to this treaty.

Because of the many different treaties to which the United States is a party, you should consult with an intellectual property lawyer to determine the appropriate notice to be used.

FILING AN APPLICATION AND DEPOSITING THE WORK

Registration with the Copyright Office is not a prerequisite for protection under the federal copyright law. The Copyright Revision Act of 1976 requires registration *only:*

1. As a prerequisite to commencing an infringement action
2. When the copyright owner wishes to take advantage of the three copyright-saving provisions (discussed in the Notice section of this chapter)
3. If the Register of Copyrights demands registration of published works bearing a copyright notice

The Berne Convention does not eliminate registration, but provides that registration is not required by copyright proprietors in other Berne signatory nations.

The current law separates registration from deposit requirements. Under the 1909 Act, filing an application for copyright registration with the Copyright Office involved paying a $6 fee and depositing two copies of the work itself (or two photographs of the original). However, "fine prints" came within the requirement of submitting two actual prints. The law now recognizes the economic hardship this caused artists and the fact that many artists intentionally failed to take advantage of copyright protection because of the burdensome deposit requirements. The Register of Copyrights is allowed to exempt certain categories from the deposit requirements or provide for alternative forms of deposit.

A craftsmaker should deposit two of the "best" copies of the work to be copyrighted with the Library of Congress within three months of publication. If the objects are bulky, fragile, or valuable, photographs may be deposited instead of the actual work. The application and the filing fee, which is now $30, need not be submitted with the copies. The Register of Copyrights can demand these copies even if there is no registration. Failure to respond to this demand can result in a $250 fine for each unsubmitted work plus the retail price of acquisition of a copy of the work. A repeated or willful failure to comply can result in a $2,500 fine.

Although you can delay registration, there are at least two reasons why a craftsmaker should deposit the work and register the copyright within three months of publication. The first is that the copyright law prohibits the awarding of attorney fees and statutory damages for infringements that occur prior to registration. This means that you can recover only actual damages if the work that is infringed is not registered before the infringement occurs.

The second reason is that, if you deposit the required two copies within the three-month period but fail to register, the Copyright Office will require two more copies of the work when you eventually do send in the registration form and filing fee.

The copyright in the work is registered once you receive back the form you submitted to the Copyright Office with a stamped registration number. Store this document in a safe place. It is your official record of registration, and you will need to produce it in the event of litigation for infringement.

Copyright laws are extremely beneficial for craftsmakers who can take advantage of them. Since the protection is simple to obtain and the cost of copyright registration is relatively low, craftsmakers should devote some attention to this means of protection.

Readers who desire more information should contact the Copyright Office, Library of Congress, Washington, D.C. 20559, or visit the Copyright Office's comprehensive Web site at *www.copyright.gov*. The registration form you will need is form "VA."

INFRINGEMENT

Copyright infringement is the unauthorized use of any of the exclusive rights protected through copyright. The federal courts have exclusive jurisdiction over copyright infringement. Actions must be brought within three years of the infringement—regardless of when the infringement is discovered. The trial judge has wide discretion in setting damages. Under the 1976 Act, as amended, the judge can award actual or, if the copyright in the work was pre-registered, statutory damages. The statutory damages range from as little as $200 for an innocent infringement to between $750 and $30,000 for the unintentional case, and up to $150,000 if the infringement is willful. The Act allows the awarding of reasonable attorney fees to the prevailing party when the copyright was registered before the infringement and provides for an injunction against continued infringement. Criminal prosecution is also theoretically available; however, it is quite uncommon—though the 2005 amendment to the copyright statute provides for more extensive criminal prosecution in some instances.

In order to prove infringement, the copyright owner must prove that: (1) the work was copyrighted and registered prior to suit being filed, (2) the infringer had access to the work and used it in the creation of the infringing work, and (3) the infringer copied a "substantial and material" portion of the protected work. Even before trial, the copyright owner may be able to obtain an order that allows the court to seize the alleged infringing works. After the trial, if infringement is established, the infringing works may be destroyed and an injunction issued against the defendant prohibiting future infringement.

FAIR USE

Not every copying of a protected work is an infringement. There are two basic types of noninfringing use—*fair use* and *exempted use*.

The 2005 amendment to the copyright statute provides libraries with the ability to reproduce "orphan" works for the libraries collection. An *orphan work* is defined as a copyrighted work that is in its last twenty years of protection and is no longer commonly available or on the market for a reasonable price.

The 1976 Act recognizes that copies of a protected work "for purposes such as criticism, comment, news reporting, teaching (including multiple copies for classroom use), scholarship, or research" can be considered fair use and not an infringement. This is not a complete list of accepted uses, nor is it intended as a definition of fair use. In addition, the Act cites four criteria to be considered in determining whether a particular use is or is not fair:

1. The purpose and character of the use, including whether such use is of a commercial nature or is for nonprofit educational purposes
2. The nature of the copyrighted work
3. The amount and substantiality of the portion used in relation to the copyrighted work as a whole
4. The effect of the use upon the potential market for or value of the copyrighted work.

The Act does not rank these four criteria, nor does it exclude other factors in determining the question of fair use. In effect, all that the Act does is leave the doctrine of fair use to be developed by the courts.

The United States Supreme Court addressed the fair use doctrine in the realm of motion pictures in *Sony Corporation of America v. Universal Studios, Inc.* The plaintiff movie producers claimed that the defendant, Sony, was enabling consumers to violate the copyright law by selling home videotape recorders. Consumers could record copyrighted works off the air. The plaintiffs alleged that Sony should be liable for copyright infringement as a conspirator. The Court concluded that home video recording for noncommercial uses is a fair use of copyrighted material. The majority of the justices expressly refrained from considering the fair use doctrine in connection with other copyrighted works. The issues raised in the *Sony* case have recently been reconsidered by the United States Supreme Court in MGM *v.* Grokster, which involved downloading protected works from the Internet.

In *American Geophysical Union v. Texaco, Inc.*, the U.S. Court of Appeals held that making even one copy of a copyrighted professional journal for purposes of retaining an article in one's file for reference purposes was an infringement. The court pointed out that if the employees of the Texaco research lab desired additional copies of articles in the copyrighted journals, reprints could have been purchased. The making of an unauthorized copy deprived the copyright owner of a sale and was, therefore, an infringement.

It has also been held that the mere fact that permission to quote from a copyrighted work has been requested and denied does not necessarily mean that a use will be infringing. In *Maxtone-Graham v. Burtchaell*, the defendant, a Catholic priest, requested permission to quote from the plaintiff's book of interviews with women who were, as the title suggests, *Pregnant by Mistake*. Since the priest's intended use of the quoted material was to support his pro-life publication, permission was denied. He, nevertheless, used the excerpts. In the resulting litigation, the court held that the use was "fair" since the priest's unauthorized use of the copyrighted material was a "productive" use and since the plaintiff was not necessarily deprived of sales.

It is, therefore, still relatively unclear how broad or narrow the scope of the fair use doctrine really is. When it is not clear that use of another's copyrighted work will be considered fair use, before you use that work, you should obtain written permission to do so. For a sample letter requesting that permission, see appendix D.

PATENT LAW AND TRADE SECRET PROTECTION

Ordinarily, before a craft can achieve a market edge, something must distinguish it from other items in the same general category. Of course, you will want to protect that "something" that sets your crafts object apart so that others cannot exploit its uniqueness. Several bodies of law may help you obtain this protection.

The copyright law, discussed in chapter 10, grants to the creator of an original work of authorship that is reduced to tangible form the right to prevent others from copying that work. But copyright protection is not granted to items of utility. Thus, if a craftsperson produces decoratively-carved brick or block for use in an archway, no matter how beautiful, creative, original, or well executed, it is not likely to be protectable under the copyright laws of the United States.

PATENT PROTECTION

Such utilitarian objects may, however, be granted protection under the *design patent* laws. For example, the design of a particular sofa or chair may be granted a design patent, even though only the aesthetic and not the utilitarian features are protectable. Similarly, a *utility patent*, the one with which you are probably most familiar, may be obtained for any new and unique process, formula, or invention that is a substantial technological innovation.

Unfortunately, patents are quite costly and difficult to obtain. It often takes an inordinate period of time for a patent document to be issued, and the period of protection is comparatively short (only twenty years from the date of application for utility patents and fourteen years for design patents).

INTERNATIONAL PATENTS

Generally speaking, each country administers its own patent system. The businessperson who wishes to obtain a foreign patent protection must, therefore, file for patents in each desired country. One exception to this rule is the European Patent Regime. Although the European Patent Office is located in Munich, European patents can be filed in any country in Europe. Once a European Patent is obtained in any member country, the patent can be translated into the language of any other European country, and, by filing it in that country, a patent may be obtained for that country without going through a separate examination process. Americans frequently file their European patents in England so they can prosecute their patents in the English language.

TRADE SECRETS

Another form of protection, known as *trade secret law*, allows exploitation of a particular innovation and may afford even greater protection than the copyright or patent laws. A trade secret may be loosely defined as anything that has not been revealed and could give you a competitive advantage. The secret should cover something that you actually use in your business and that you take some reasonable steps to protect. A trade secret may be lost if the owner fails to identify it as a trade secret or proprietary information or fails to take reasonable steps to protect it. Otherwise, the trade secret protection is perpetual.

All that is necessary for something to be protectable as a trade secret is that:

1. It gives the possessor a competitive advantage
2. It will, in fact, be treated as a secret by you
3. It is not generally known in your industry or business

The fundamental question of trade secret law is, *What is protectable?* The way you use knowledge and information and the specific portions of information you have grouped together may themselves be trade secrets, even if everything you consider important for your secrets is publicly available information. For example, if there are numerous methods for producing a particular dye and you have selected one of them, the mere fact that you have selected this method may itself be a trade secret. The identity of your suppliers may be a trade secret, even if they are all listed in the yellow pages. The fact that you have done business with these people and found them to be reputable and responsive to you may make the list of their names a trade secret.

Many trade secrets will be embodied in some form of document. One of the first things you should do is to mark any paper, photograph, or the like, identifying it as *confidential*. You should also take steps to prevent demonstrations of your trade secret, such as manufacturing methods. Taking these steps will not create trade secret protection, but should litigation ever arise, the fact that an effort has been made to identify the materials and methods you consider secret will aid you in establishing that you treat them as a trade secret. In this area, a little thought and cleverness will go a long way toward giving you the protection of the trade secret laws.

You should also have some degree of physical security. It has been said that physical security is 90 percent common sense and 10 percent true protection. Restrict access to an area in which your trade secret is used. For instance, some precaution should be taken to prevent visitors from peering into the manufacturing area where the secret process, formula, or technique is employed. The credentials of delivery and service persons should be examined, as the donning of a disguise to gain entry into a restricted area is a favorite ploy of business spies. Employee access to trade secret information should be on a *need-to-know* basis; employees should not be automatically granted free access to the material you desire to keep as a trade secret.

As noted above, documents containing trade secrets should be clearly labeled, as should pictures, sketches, and the like. A procedure should be established for controlling employee access to the documents. For instance, one person could be responsible for granting access to trade secret materials, and a sign-in/sign-out process or the like could be instituted for those permitted access to such documents.

If possible, the information that you consider to be a trade secret should be fragmented. This means that no one employee should have possession of the entire secret; thus, no one person will have sufficient information to hurt you.

It is also a good idea to have employees sign a confidentiality and nondisclosure agreement when they are hired or change responsibilities. An attorney who deals with intellectual property can prepare form agreements for use within your business. A sample form is set forth in appendix C(6).

If it ever becomes important for you to reveal a secret to an outsider, such as when someone desires to purchase the right to exploit your innovation through a licensing arrangement, a confidentiality agreement is in order. These agreements generally provide that in exchange for disclosure of the confidential trade secret information, the party receiving such information will keep it in confidence and will not use it without the express written permission of the person making the disclosure. Again, your intellectual property lawyer can prepare such an agreement for you. A sample form can be found in appendix C(6).

Another method of protecting your trade secret is to engage in some vague labeling. For example, if your trade secret consists of a unique mixture for a glaze, then instead of having the components of the glaze bear their true names, label them "Ingredient A," "Ingredient B," and "Ingredient C." Then, if an employee quits or if a stranger happens into your office, all that will be known is that by mixing some portion of A with some portion of B, combined with some portion of C, the desired result will be achieved. This will not be very useful information. Similarly, if the trade secret is the temperature at which a glaze is fired, you may wish to have the original temperature marks removed and replaced by colored zones.

If you are publishing in or contributing to trade journals or crafts publications, take care not to reveal trade secrets. Occasionally, manufacturers or their employees inadvertently disclose valuable information in an attempt to impress their colleagues.

In order to avoid the charge that you are stealing someone else's trade secret, you should question employees who come to work for you from a competitor. If there is any possibility of the new employee using the competitor's trade secret information, the new employee should meet with the former employer and attempt to obtain written permission to use that information while working for you.

Trade secret laws may be the only protection available for your crafts business secrets. Care should, therefore, be taken to restrict access to such information and to treat that information as truly secret. Contractual arrangements with both employees and outsiders are quite useful. These, coupled with your common sense in the day-to-day operation of your crafts business, will go a long way toward protecting your intellectual property.

PATENT OR PADLOCK DILEMMA

The determination as to whether patent or trade secret protection is most appropriate is sometimes referred to as the "patent or padlock dilemma." It is not possible to obtain both kinds of protection, since achieving one will render the other meaningless. The patent-versus-padlock decision must be made within one year after discovery, since the patent laws provide that a patent can be obtained only when the invention in question has not been in public use for more than one year before an application is made. Furthermore, use by the inventor for commercial purposes, even in secret, is considered a "public use" within the meaning of the patent law.

Thus, during the first year, the inventor must decide how the innovation will be protected. If trade secret protection is selected, then patent protection is probably lost forever. Selecting a patent is also exclusive, because it destroys trade secret protection, since the patent application must contain a full description of precisely what was invented. Once issued, *letters patent* will disclose the invention to the public.

As you can see, it is impossible to both obtain a patent and to reserve some aspect of the invention as secret. The patent application itself is not public information, however. An applicant may withdraw the application at any time before letters patent are issued without jeopardizing trade secret protection.

In order to determine which of these methods of protection should be elected, you should consult an attorney who specializes in intellectual property. See chapter 16, How to Find a Lawyer.

LICENSING

I f someone likes your crafts work and wishes to duplicate it, you can exploit your own intellectual property by granting the other person a *license*.

A license to use your copyright, trademark, trade dress, or patent should be in writing. It should describe the scope of the user's permission: how long the license will last, whether the user can market copies throughout the world or only in specific locations, whether the license allows exploitation of the entire intellectual property or only a portion of it (e.g., use of a copyrighted photo on T-shirts, but not on anything else), etc.

Care should be taken when defining these boundaries. For example, if a license permits sales or other exploitation of the licensed products or technology in Canada, then Canadian sales to a business that ships the goods to the United States may be within the scope of permitted use, resulting in U.S. licensees competing with Canadian licensees for sales within the United States. This "gray market" problem can be controlled by using care in drafting license agreements.

Care should also be taken to avoid allowing your intellectual property to be exploited in countries that do not honor U.S. intellectual property laws, have laws that are less protective than ours, or have no intellectual property law at all. The U.S. State Department has a "watch list" of countries that do not honor their intellectual property treaty obligations or that have a poor record of enforcement with respect to intellectual property. You may request a copy of this list from the United States Department of State, 2201 C Street, NW, Washington, D.C. 20520, (202) 647-4000; also see *www.ustr.gov/Trade_Sectors/Intellectual_Property/Section_Index.html.*

The advent of the World Wide Web has presented a host of new challenges. Since material may be captured anywhere in the world, even in areas that may not be desirable, care should be taken in determining what is placed on the Web and whether your license permits or prohibits Web postings.

Another issue to consider is whether the licensee will be permitted to sublicense. When permitted, the right to sublicense can affect the price paid for a license. Sublicense provisions should be carefully drafted and tied directly to the terms of the original license agreement. All provisions in the original license agreement should apply to any sublicense agreements negotiated by the licensee.

METHOD OF PAYMENT

Once the decision to license has been made, the price must be negotiated. Payment for the license should be spelled out in the license agreement. You can demand a flat fee in exchange for permission to use your copyright, trademark, or patent, or you may prefer to receive some portion of the income as a royalty. This payment can either be a fixed amount per item or a percentage, perhaps 5 percent, of the money received by the person or company exploiting the right. Attention should be given to defining the specific sum the percentage will be based upon. Specify, for example, if it will be a percentage of the net receipts or the gross receipts from the sale of items covered by the license, and carefully define the term used.

Payments based on sales are referred to as *royalties*. One should be very careful to define when they are due and payable and on what basis they are to be calculated. Unfortunately, numerous unscrupulous licensees have used creative accounting to reduce their obligations.

If international transactions are involved, be sure to specify which country's currency is to be used. The value of U.S. dollars, Canadian dollars, and Australian dollars, for example, typically differ significantly, and there is a cost involved in currency conversion.

It is also important to include in a licensing agreement a provision whereby you can verify the accuracy of the records showing what is due to you. This can be accomplished by requiring the person to whom the license is granted to have an accounting report preceding or accompanying any royalty checks. If you dispute the validity of the report, there should be an agreed-upon right to have an independent accountant audit the books. Where possible, you should negotiate a provision that places the obligation for paying the outside auditor on the party rendering the accounting if an error of more than a specified percentage, typically 5 to 10 percent, of the total payment is discovered.

ACKNOWLEDGMENT OF INTELLECTUAL PROPERTY OWNERSHIP AND QUALITY OF REPRODUCTIONS

To retain the protection afforded by the patent, trademark, or copyright laws, you must require any person who uses your creation to acknowledge your ownership and include the appropriate notice on the work. It is common to see a legend that states, "Reproduced with permission of J. Jones, the copyright owner."

Since the work marketed after you have granted a license will bear your name or trademark, it will usually be difficult, if not impossible, for consumers to distinguish between your work and those works reproduced by the person to whom you have granted a license. For this reason, it is important for you to retain some degree of quality control over the licensed product. In fact, it has been held that a "naked" license of a trademark—one without quality control measures—is void. And in fact, the trademark itself may be lost. A provision in the license should, therefore, require the licensee to demonstrate some method by which the item will be reproduced and some means by which you can evaluate the quality of the final products. To cite an example on a grand scale, when the Metropolitan Museum of Art in New York obtained the right to create copies of some of the pieces displayed in the King Tut exhibit, one of the primary concerns of the Egyptian government was the quality of the reproductions.

In order for the license to be valid and enforceable, it should be signed by both parties. You should make it clear that the license is personal and may not be assigned or exploited by anyone but the person to whom it is given, unless you give your prior written permission. It is also wise to provide that the license is void and no longer in effect if any of its terms, including payment of royalties or the like, are violated. It is important to record your license in the appropriate place: the Copyright Office or the Office of the Commissioner of Patents and Trademarks, where applicable.

Lawyers who specialize in intellectual property can be helpful in explaining the myriad of options available to you through the licensing process and in drafting a document that will afford you maximum protection in granting the right to another person to exploit your intellectual property.

If the craftsperson wishes to retain title to the copyright and merely permit another to use it by producing a limited number of copies, a license may be entered into between the parties. A license is merely a permission to use the property of another and is a contract. For a form license agreement and explanation of its terms see appendix C(5a and 5b).

COMMERCIAL LEASES

A t some time in your professional life as a craftsperson, you may be in a position where you will have to evaluate the terms and conditions of a commercial lease. You may also have to examine a residential lease, although these are customarily more tightly regulated by state law than are commercial leases. The rules regulating a relationship between a landlord and a tenant vary from state to state, and it is important for you to consult with a local attorney who has some expertise in dealing with this body of law before signing a lease. You may wish to call your attorney's attention to some specific items in a commercial lease that could be of great concern to you as a craftsperson.

THE PROPERTY AND THE COST

One of the most important terms in any lease is the description of the property to be rented. Be sure that the document specifies, in some detail, the area that you are entitled to occupy. Determine whether there is a distinction between the size of the space leased and the actual area of that space that is *usable*. Often, tenants are required to pay rent on commercial space measured from "wall to wall," although, after the area is built out according to the tenant's specifications, the resulting usable space may be significantly smaller. Sometimes the term "u.s.f." (usable square feet) or a similar term is used to designate actual usable space, while the term "r.s.f." (rentable square feet) refers to the amount of space wall to wall. For example, 110 r.s.f. may be equivalent to 100 u.s.f. once that 110 r.s.f. space is built to suit the tenant's needs.

If you will be renting a storefront in a shopping center or mall with common areas, you should have the responsibilities for those common areas spelled out. Will you be responsible for cleaning and maintaining them, or will the landlord? When will the common areas be open or closed? What other facilities are available to you and/or your customers, such as restrooms, storage, and the like?

Another important item, obviously, is the cost of the leased space. Will you be paying a flat monthly rental or one that will change based on your earnings at the location? In order to evaluate the cost of the space, you should compare it with other similar spaces in the same locale. Do not be afraid to negotiate for more favorable terms. Care should be taken not to sign a lease that will restrict you from opening another crafts shop near the one being rented under this lease.

LENGTH OF THE LEASE

It is also important to consider the period of the lease. If, for example, a craftsperson rents a booth at a crafts fair, he or she will be concerned with only a short time period. On the other hand, if the craftsperson intends to rent a studio for a year or two, it is a good idea to try to get an *option to extend*. It is likely that a craftsperson will wish to advertise and promote his or her business. Obviously, if you move on an annual basis, customers who return to purchase only on an irregular basis may not know where to find you after the lease period ends. Worse still, they may find another craftsperson in your old space. Of course, your work is likely to differ from the next tenant's, but there is always a risk that the collector may purchase one of the new craftsperson's pieces rather than try to locate you at your new address.

Long-term leases are recordable in some jurisdictions. If you are in a position to record your lease, it is probably a good idea to do so, since you will then be entitled to receive legal and other notices related to the property.

RESTRICTIONS TO WATCH OUT FOR

It is essential for a craftsperson to determine whether there are any restrictions on the particular activities that may be performed on the leased premises. For example, the area may be zoned so that a kiln may not be installed. It is a good idea to insist on a provision in the lease that puts the burden of obtaining any permits or variances on the landlord or, if the craftsperson is responsible for them, allowing the craftsperson to terminate the lease without penalty if he or she is unable to obtain the necessary permits or variances.

Be sure that the lease permits the display of any signage or advertising used in connection with your crafts business. It is not uncommon, for example, for historic landmark laws to regulate the types of signs that may be placed on older buildings. Additionally, learn if signage can be placed in the shop's window or in front of the building. Some zoning laws also prohibit this.

If the place you wish to rent will be used as both your personal dwelling and for your crafts business, other problems may arise. See chapter 14 for more information.

ENVIRONMENTAL ISSUES

The federal government and most state governments have imposed environmental constraints on the use of land. You should learn what they are and whether there will be any limitations on your desired uses. For example, the Clean Air Act deals with particle emission control. Other regulatory statutes deal with waste disposal and the like.

REMODELING AND UTILITIES

Craftspeople should also be aware that extensive remodeling may be necessary for certain spaces to become useful galleries or studios. If this is the case, it is important to determine who will be responsible for the costs of remodeling. The landlord may be willing to pay for all the tenant improvements or the expense of tenant improvements up to some agreed-upon amount. In addition, it is essential to find out whether it will be necessary for you to restore the premises to their original condition when the lease ends. This can be extraordinarily expensive and, in some instances, impossible to accomplish.

Another consideration when building out a space for a crafts shop or gallery area is the Americans with Disabilities Act of 1990 (ADA), which requires places of public accommodation to be reasonably accessible. The law is broadly interpreted and includes virtually every type of business. The term "reasonable accommodation" is not precise, and thus it is important to determine what must be done in order to fulfill the requirements of this federal statute. Typically, approximately 25 percent of the cost of any covered remodel must be allocated to items that aid accessibility. These would include, among other things, levered door openers, Braille signs, larger bathroom stalls, wheelchair ramps, approved disabled-accessible doors, and elevators. You should determine whether the cost of complying with the ADA will be imposed on the landlord, on the tenant, or be divided between the two, and if divided, the proportion of costs for which each party will be responsible.

If your crafts shop will need special hookups, such as water or electrical lines that are not already available in the space, find out whether the landlord will provide them or whether you have to bear the cost of having them brought in. If the landlord will assume some or all of the cost of these utilities, they may become part of the total amount spent on tenant improvements.

The lease you sign should also spell out whether the costs of these utilities will be included in the rent or if are they to be paid separately.

Additionally, in some locations, garbage pickup is not a problem, since it is one of the services provided by the municipality. On the other hand, it is common for renters to be responsible for their own trash disposal. In commercial spaces, this can be quite expensive and should also be addressed in the lease.

INSURANCE, SECURITY, AND DELIVERIES

Customarily, the landlord will be responsible for the exterior of the building. It should be the landlord's obligation to make sure that it does not leak during rainstorms and that it is properly ventilated. Nevertheless, it is important that the lease deals with the question of this responsibility in case, for example, the building is damaged and some of your crafts or materials are harmed or destroyed.

Will you have to take out insurance for the building, as well as its contents, or will the landlord assume responsibility for such insurance? Similarly, find out whether you will have to get liability insurance for injuries sustained in portions of the building not under your control, such as common areas, hallways, and the like. In any case, you should, of course, have your own liability policy for accidental injuries or accidents that occur on your premises.

A good lease will also contain a provision dealing with security. If you are renting an internal space in a shopping center, it is likely that the landlord will be responsible for external security. This is not universally the case, though, so you should find out about security. If you are renting an entire building, it is customarily your responsibility to provide whatever security you deem important. Does the lease permit you to install locks or alarm systems? If this is something in which you are going to be interested, you should make sure that it does.

Many craftspeople have materials delivered to the gallery during off hours so as to avoid disturbing the operation of the building. Does the lease have any restrictions regarding time or location of deliveries? If you are dealing with large bulky items and are accepting deliveries or making them, put a provision in your lease that will give you the flexibility you desire.

GET IT IN WRITING

Finally, it is essential to be sure that every item agreed upon between you and the landlord is in writing. This is particularly important when dealing with leases, since many state laws provide that a long-term lease is an interest in land and can only be enforced if it is in writing.

The relationship between landlords and tenants is an ancient one that is currently undergoing a good deal of change. Care should be taken when examining a location to determine exactly what you can or can't do on the premises and whether the landlord or municipal rules will allow you to use the location for your specific purpose.

WORKING AT HOME

I t is extremely common for artists and craftspeople to have studios or workshops in a home or garage. This is true for a variety of reasons, including the desire to be able to work whenever one has the urge, regardless of the hour. The most important reason, though, is probably one of economics. The cost of renting a separate studio or workshop can be prohibitive. Not too many artists and craftspeople are willing or able to pay it. Others, of course, choose to work at home because it enables them to juggle work and family obligations.

The problems raised by the multiple use of a dwelling can be divided into two basic areas, namely, whether the income tax laws recognize the realities of the arts-and-crafts world, and whether local zoning regulations allow you to legally work and live in the same place.

TAX CONSIDERATIONS

First, let us examine whether and how craftspeople can obtain tax deductions for the use of their homes as their businesses.

For some time, the IRS did not allow deductions for offices or studios in homes. This policy was challenged in a case in which a physician managed rental properties as a sideline. The doctor's rental business was run out of an office in his house, and the space was used only for this particular business. When the physician deducted the expenses for the office in his home, the IRS disallowed the deduction. The court, however, was apparently convinced by the physical setup of the room that the doctor used it exclusively and regularly as an office in connection with his rental business. The court noted, for example, that the room had no television set, sofa, or bed.

This decision has now been incorporated into the Tax Code. As a general rule, a business deduction is not allowed for the use of a dwelling that is used by the taxpayer during the taxable year as a residence. There are some technical rules regarding qualification of a dwelling as a residence. The Code makes an exception to this general rule in certain circumstances, allowing the taxpayer to take a deduction for a portion of a dwelling unit "exclusively used on a regular basis . . . as a principal place of business for any trade or business of the taxpayer," even if that business is not the taxpayer's primary source of income.

Exclusive and Regular Use

Some craftspeople may be able to satisfy one or more of the exceptions to this rule. The first exception is for any portion of the residence used *exclusively* and *on a regular basis* as the craftsperson's *principal place of business* or as a place to meet clients or customers. The requirement of exclusivity means that the taxpayer may not mix personal use and business use. In other words, a taxpayer may not deduct expenses for a studio if it is also used as a storeroom for personal belongings, a guest room, or the like.

There has, however, been a recent liberalization of this rule in some parts of the country, where courts have held that a studio or an office can exist in a room that has a personal use so long as a clearly defined area is used exclusively for business. It is important to remember that, generally, the Internal Revenue Service functions on a regional basis. Except for issues that have been reserved for decision by the National Office, each IRS office is independent and makes its own decisions until the United States Supreme Court or Congress makes a decision that applies nationally. That is why a decision by a circuit court in one area may not apply elsewhere.

The requirement regarding regularity means that the use of the room may not be merely incidental or occasional. Obviously, there is a gray area between *regular* and *occasional*. Perhaps some artists or craftspeople can use this rule as an inducement to overcome temporary bouts of laziness or boredom. If you plan to deduct any expenses for your studio, you must keep working to satisfy the regularity test.

Like the regularity requirement, the rule regarding the *principal place of business* has been interpreted differently by different courts. In 1993, the Supreme Court resolved these ambiguities by holding, in *Soliman v. Commissioner*, that home-office deductions were not available where the taxpayer performed the services or delivered goods outside of the home and income was thus not directly generated at home.

The Taxpayer Relief Act of 1997, effective in 1999, expanded the definition of a taxpayer's principal place of business to include the place where administrative and management activities are conducted if there is no other fixed location for the accomplishment of such tasks. For instance, an artist who creates artwork in a rented studio space could take the deduction for an office at home if the administrative aspects of the business, such as contacting galleries regarding sales, ordering supplies, and the like, were conducted from the home office.

When the studio is in a structure separate from the principal residence, the requirements for deductibility are less stringent. The structure must be used exclusively and on a regular basis, just as a studio in the home itself. However, when the studio is in a separate structure, the studio need only be used "in connection with" the artistic business, not as the principal place of business.

When craftspeople use portions of their homes for storage purposes, the requirements for deductibility are also less stringent. The dwelling must be the sole fixed location of the business and must be used on a regular basis for the storage of the craftsperson's works or materials. The entire room used for storage need not be used exclusively for business, but there must be a "separately identifiable space suitable for storage" of the craftsperson's works or materials.

When a craftsperson is employed by another in his or her professional capacity as a craftsperson, a deduction for the home studio is more difficult to justify. In addition to fulfilling the tests outlined above, the employee's use of the home studio must be "for the convenience of his employer." This test would not be met if the employer provides a studio for his or her employees.

Are the Deductions Worthwhile?

If a craftsperson meets one of the tests outlined above, the next question is, What tax benefits can result? After close analysis, the answer is frequently, Not very many. An *allocable portion* of mortgage interest and property taxes can be deducted against the business, but these would be deductible anyway if the taxpayer itemizes. The advantage of deducting them against the business is that this reduces the business profit that is subject to self-employment taxes.

Of course, a taxpayer who rents a house and otherwise qualifies for the deductions may deduct a portion of the rent that would not otherwise be tax-deductible. The primary tax advantage comes from the ability to deduct an allocable portion of repairs, utility bills, and depreciation.

To arrive at the allocable portion, take the square footage of the space used for the business and divide that by the total square footage of the house. Multiply this fraction by the sum of your mortgage interest, property taxes, and other deductible expenses for the amount to be deducted from the business. The procedure used to determine the amount of allowable depreciation is too complex an issue to discuss here and should be reviewed with your tax advisor.

The total amount that can be deducted for a studio or storage place in the home is artificially limited. To determine the amount that can be deducted, take the total amount of money earned in the business and subtract the business deductions allowed for supplies, salaries, and the like, as well as the allocable portion of mortgage interest and property taxes. The remainder is the maximum amount that you can deduct for the allocable portion of repairs, utilities, and depreciation. In other words, your total business deductions in this situation cannot be greater than your total business income.

If this number is negative, there is no deduction allowed. Taxpayers are allowed to carry forward any deductions for home-office use that are not allowed because of the gross-income limit and deduct such amounts against profits in future years.

The IRS has also determined that a taxpayer cannot deduct any charges, including excise and sales taxes, that are paid to obtain phone service for the *first* residential phone line. This means that a taxpayer with a single phone line cannot deduct any charges that could otherwise be allocable to business use. The same principle would likely apply to Internet and cell phone service.

Besides the obvious complexity of the rules and the mathematics, there are several other factors that limit the benefit of taking a deduction for a studio in the home. One of these is the partial loss of the *non-recognition of gain* (tax-deferred) treatment that is otherwise allowed when a taxpayer sells a personal residence. The Tax Relief Act of 1997 allows homeowners to exclude up to $250,000 of the gain ($500,000 for joint filers) from income with some restrictions. This deferral of gain, however, is not allowed to the extent that the house was used in the business. This means that the taxpayer must pay tax on the allocable portion of the gain from the sale.

Example: If you have been claiming 20 percent of your home as a business deduction, when you sell the home, you will enjoy a tax deferral on only 80 percent of the profit. The other 20 percent will be subject to tax because that 20 percent represents the sale of a business asset. In essence, for the price of a current deduction, you may be converting what is essentially a tax-deferred asset into business property. Some of that 20 percent may be excluded if you have both (1) owned the home for two of the last five years and (2) used the home exclusively for personal use for two of the last five years. If both of these requirements are met, tax must be paid only on the amount actually deducted for depreciation.

If you plan to sell anytime soon, you should confer with your tax advisor.

Another negative factor is that by deducting for a studio in the home, the taxpayer in effect puts a red flag on his or her tax return. Obviously, when the tax return expressly asks whether expenses are being deducted for an office in the home, the question is not being asked for purely academic reasons. Although only the IRS knows how much the answer to this question affects someone's chances of being audited, there is little doubt that a "yes" answer does increase the likelihood of an audit.

Given this increased possibility of audit, it does not pay to deduct for a studio in the home in doubtful situations. Taxpayers who lose the deduction must pay back taxes plus interest and, possibly, penalties.

If you believe that your home studio or workshop could qualify for the business deduction, you would be well advised to consult with a competent tax expert who can assist in calculating the deduction.

LEGAL CONSIDERATIONS

Let us turn now to some of the legal considerations involved in living and working in the same space. Local zoning ordinances and federal labor regulations can all have an affect on such a setup. In some instances, this may make working at home less attractive than it might otherwise seem. In evaluating the feasibility of working at home, craftspeople will need to consider the effects of several different laws.

Local Zoning Restrictions

For the craftsperson who wants to live and work in the same space, local zoning ordinances can be a significant factor. Some city and county ordinances flatly prohibit using the same space as both a business and a dwelling. In some commercially zoned areas where craftspeople can rent low-cost lofts and studios, it is illegal to maintain a residence in the same space. In residential areas, the craftsperson may have to comply with regulations that require permits and restrict the size and use of the studio.

Municipal and county ordinances vary, and the craftsmaker should, therefore, check with the appropriate local government agency or agencies to determine specific requirements. The fire department, for example, will undoubtedly have to approve the use of a kiln.

For the craftsperson who wants to maintain a studio or workshop in the garage or basement of a residence, several types of restrictions may apply. The space devoted to the crafts activity may be limited to a certain number of square feet, and outbuildings may or may not be allowed. The type of equipment used may also be restricted. Noise, smoke, and odor restrictions may apply, and the craftsperson may have to obtain approval from all or some of the neighbors. If remodeling is contemplated, building permits may be required and building codes must be observed.

The craftsperson also may have to obtain a home occupation permit or, in many jurisdictions, a business license. The application fee for either of these will normally be a flat fee or a percentage of annual receipts from the activity. Depending upon the success of the business, this can be a substantial expense. In addition, the craftsmaker's, home-owner's, or renter's insurance policy may contain some restrictions on commercial activity. The craftsperson should, therefore, contact his or her insurance broker to find out whether such limitations exist and what can be done about them.

In commercially zoned areas, craftspeople may have more flexibility in the types of activities they conduct, particularly if the craft produces noise or odors that would be offensive to others in a residential location. If the craftsmaker also wishes to use the workspace for eating and sleeping, zoning ordinances may prohibit such use.

Some cities have recognized the hardships these zoning ordinances create for artists and craftspeople. In New York City, for example, a municipal dwelling law was enacted exempting artists and their families from restrictions against living and working in the same apartment unit. The state of California also has enacted legislation that grants local municipalities the right to adopt zoning ordinances that would accommodate artists who live in industrially or commercially zoned areas. You should check with your local municipal authority to determine whether it has adopted laws or regulations that would allow you to create your crafts in the same space in which you live.

While these laws solved the immediate problem of artists and crafts-people living and working in the same location, new problems were created. For example, once it became possible for artists to live and work in the SoHo district of New York City, the area became a magnet for galleries, boutiques, restaurants, and tourists. Many artists remain, but many had to move, having been forced out by skyrocketing rents and prices.

Before SoHo became fashionable, no new industry could be enticed into the area. Consequently, landlords were pleased to have artists leasing their commercial property. Once development caught on, however, buildings changed hands more often, and artists and craftspeople who had invested substantial sums in their lofts found that their commercial leases afforded them little protection from substantial, unanticipated increases in rent. This same pattern is now occurring in the Pearl District of my hometown, Portland, Oregon.

A 1979 New York case, *Mandel v. Pitkowsky*, may provide residential-loft tenants with some degree of security. Pitkowsky and sculptor Ulrich Niemeyer had rented commercial quarters for ten years. Their lease limited their occupancy to an artist's studio. Nevertheless, their landlord encouraged them to convert the studio into their residence. Both sides were happy to abide by this illegal arrangement, apparently secure in the knowledge that the city was not diligently inspecting these properties.

When the lease expired, however, the landlord demanded a threefold increase in the rent. The landlord claimed that because the property was commercial rather than residential, it was not subject to the city's rent-stabilization laws. The court did not agree. The landlord's express approval of the tenants' ten-year residency converted the studio into a *de facto* multiple dwelling for purposes of the rent-stabilization laws.

Federal Regulations

Federal laws that inhibit cottage industries can also adversely affect craftspeople who want to work at home. For almost fifty years, the U.S. Department of Labor actively enforced a 1943 regulation prohibiting individuals from producing six categories of crafts in their homes: embroidery, women's apparel, gloves and mittens, buttons and buckles, jewelry, and handkerchiefs. The Department of Labor was primarily concerned with violations of the minimum-wage provisions of the Fair Labor Standards Act, which requires employers to pay their employees no less than a set minimum hourly wage. Some states may have a higher minimum wage, and whenever state law requires a higher minimum wage, the higher wage must be paid. Overtime pay, at one-and-one-half times the hourly rate, is mandated for hours worked over forty hours per week.

In 1982, the Department of Labor repealed the prohibition on knitted outerwear; however, it faced bitter union opposition. Eight years later, in 1989, the prohibitions on the remaining five categories were lifted, although, in the case of jewelry, the prohibition was lifted only for non-hazardous jewelry work. This greatly decreases the difficulties that have faced home craftsworkers in the past.

The remaining regulations may still create serious difficulties for people who want to work at home. In recent years, the disputes between labor unions, principally the International Ladies Garment Workers Union, and those who make their living from cottage industries has become quite heated. The unions argue that they merely want to prevent sweatshop conditions, but many people believe that the real issue is nonunionized home labor competing with union members who work in factories.

In order to fall within the scope of the regulation, the worker must be an employee. This does not mean, however, that a person can avoid the effect of the regulation simply by labeling himself or herself as an independent contractor. Under the Fair Labor Standards Act, the test of employment is the economic reality of the relationship. For example, the Supreme Court has held that members of a cooperative may be employees for the purposes of the home-worker regulation. The decision was based on several factors, including the fact that the cooperative's management decided the work to be performed and who was to do it. The management also decided who could become a member of the cooperative and could terminate the relationship if a member's work was substandard.

At the other end of the spectrum are manufacturers who are self-employed and independent, selling their products on the open market wholesale or retail for whatever price they can command. In this situation, the federal regulations do not apply. But what the Department of Labor has lifted, it can re-impose if "significant wage or other violations" are found among homeworkers. Craftspeople should be aware that these or similar regulations may reappear.

If you are a craftsperson leasing space for your business or if, rather than owning your home, you are renting it with the understanding that a portion will be used as a crafts studio, you should be prepared to negotiate a commercial-style lease. For an explanation of commercial leases, see chapter 13.

LABOR RELATIONS

There comes a time in almost every craftsperson's life when it is necessary to get help, be it brain or brawn. The help most commonly needed is a bookkeeper or accountant who can handle taxes, billing, and the like. When things get a little hectic around the shop or studio, you might hire someone to help with packing or running errands. If selling is not your greatest talent, you may engage the services of a salesperson or a manufacturer's representative. Simply stated, the higher your sales volume, the less likely you will be able to do it all yourself.

INDEPENDENT CONTRACTORS

When you hire someone on a one-time or job-by-job basis, that person is called an *independent contractor*. Although you pay for their services, such people remain their own bosses and may even subcontract others to actually do the work for you. For a form agreement that may be used to retain the services of an independent contractor, see appendix C(7).

If you occasionally give some of your work to a friend to sell on consignment at a crafts fair, the friend would probably be an independent contractor. If once or twice a year, you hire a bookkeeper or accountant to go over your records, that person, too, is an independent contractor. The fact that the person is independent and not your employee means that you do not have to pay Social Security taxes in addition to the cost of the work, nor do you have to withhold income taxes or comply with the other rules imposed on employers.

More importantly, if someone is injured while working for you, as a result of the independent contractor's negligence, you will generally be immune from liability. There are, however, situations where you are legally responsible for the independent contractor's wrongful acts. Such situations fall into three basic categories:

1. If an employer is careless in hiring an independent contractor and a careful investigation would have disclosed facts to indicate that the contractor was not qualified, the employer may be liable when the independent contractor fails to properly perform the job.
2. If a job is so dangerous as to be characterized as "ultrahazardous" (a legal term) and is to be performed for the employer's benefit, then, regardless of who performs the work, the employer will remain legally responsible for any injuries that occur during the performance of the work. Thus, a fireworks displayer, for example, cannot escape liability by having fuses lit or rockets aimed by independent contractors.
3. An employer may be required by law to perform certain tasks for the health and safety of the community. This responsibility is said to be *nondelegable*—that is, an employer cannot delegate such tasks and thus escape liability for their improper performance. If, therefore, a nondelegable duty is performed by an independent contractor, the employer will remain responsible for any injury that results.

A good example of a nondelegable duty is the law (common in many states) that homeowners are responsible for keeping their sidewalks free of dangerous obstacles. If a homeowner hires an independent contractor to fulfill this obligation by removing ice during the winter, the home-owner may still be legally liable to someone injured on the slippery sidewalk, even if the accident resulted from the contractor's carelessness.

EMPLOYEES

The other capacity in which someone can work for you is that of *employee*. This category includes anyone over whose work you exercise direct control. Helpers, apprentices, and salespeople who represent you alone, a bookkeeper who works full-time, and regular part-time members of your staff are examples.

The formation of this relationship entails nothing more than an agreement on your side to hire someone and an agreement by that person to work for you. Although a written contract is not necessary, except in the case of employment for more than one year, I suggest that employment terms be put down in writing so that there is no misunderstanding later.

Employment Contracts

If the employment is to be for more than one year, there must be a written contract specifying the period of employment; otherwise, either party may terminate the relationship at any time. While there is no prescribed form that the contract must take, there are, nevertheless, certain items that should be considered.

The first item of an employment contract is the term of employment. An employment contract may be either terminable "at will" or for a fixed duration. Making the contract for a fixed period gives the employee some job security and creates a moral and contractual obligation for the employee to remain for the term. Of course, if the employee chooses to quit or the employer chooses to fire the employee, the law will not compel fulfillment of the contract. Improper termination of a contract for a fixed period, however, will cause the party who is responsible for the wrongful act to be liable for damages.

The second item is the wage. Unless you are a large employer with forty-five or more employees or are engaged in interstate commerce (which is defined as having gross sales of $500,000 or more), you will not have to comply with federal minimum-wage laws. Most states however, have their own minimum-wage laws with which you still must comply. Other than the requirement imposed by this law, the amount of remuneration is open to bargaining.

In addition to an hourly wage or monthly salary, other benefits can be given, such as health and life insurance or retirement pensions. Some legal advice may be necessary here in order to take advantage of tax laws. In the event no salary is specified, the law will presume a reasonable wage for the work performed. Thus, you cannot escape paying your employees fairly by not discussing the amount they will earn. If you hire a glassblower and the accepted salary in your region for a person qualified to blow glass is $10 per hour, then it is presumed that the glassblower is hired for this amount unless you and that person have agreed to a different salary.

Third, it is often wise to spell out your employee's duties in the employment contract. This serves as a form of orientation for the employee and also may limit future conflicts over what is and what is not involved in the job.

Fourth, you may want your employee to agree not to work for someone else while working for you or, more importantly, not to compete with you after the end of the employment period. The latter agreement must be carefully drawn to be enforceable. Such an agreement must not be overly broad in the kind of work the employee may not do, it must cover a geographic area no broader than that in which you actually operate, and it must be for a reasonable duration—a three-year period has been upheld.

Note that some states impose restrictions on noncompetition agreements. In Oregon, for example, a noncompetition agreement is unenforceable unless it was entered into either prior to or contemporaneously with the beginning of employment, or upon a meaningful promotion. Some states refuse to uphold noncompetition agreements. For example, California law states that a noncompetition agreement is generally void as against public policy.

Employers may achieve some form of protection by restricting their intellectual property. This should include a prohibition on the use of any company trade secrets, both during the term of employment and thereafter. These restrictions should be in writing. It has been held that trade secrets may include, among other things, customer lists, supplier lists, secret formulas, know-how, and the like.

Finally, grounds for termination of the employment contract should be listed, even if the contract is terminable at will, in which event you should clearly specify that the contract may be terminated either for the specified causes or at the will of the employer.

You are liable for the negligence and, sometimes, even the intentional wrongdoing of your employee when the employee is acting on your behalf. This means that if your employee is on the job and is involved in an automobile accident that is his or her fault, you, as well as your employee, may be legally liable. It would be wise to be extremely careful when hiring and to contact your insurance agent to obtain sufficient insurance coverage for your additional exposure. For an example of an employment agreement form and a form that may be used for the purpose of making it clear that employment may be terminated at anytime by either the employer or employee, see appendix C(8 and 9).

Other Considerations in Hiring

There are other issues you should consider when hiring an employee, most of which fall into the realm of accounting or bookkeeping responsibilities. You should, therefore, consult with your accountant or bookkeeper regarding such items as the following:

- A workers' compensation policy for your employees in the event of on-the-job injury or occupational illness. State laws vary on the minimum number of employees an employer must have before it is required to obtain such a policy. The workers' compensation laws of many states provide that an employer who has failed to obtain or keep in force required workers' compensation insurance will be strictly liable, even in the absence of negligence, for on-the-job injuries or illnesses, including not only medical expenses but also damages for pain and suffering, lost earning potential, and other damages that are a consequence of on-the-job injuries or illnesses.

- Withholding taxes (federal, state, and local). Here, too, the laws vary, and you are urged to find out what is required in your locale.
- Social Security (FICA). There are some exemptions from this body of social legislation. Contact your local Social Security office to determine how these exemptions may affect you.
- Unemployment insurance (both federal and state). These also include certain technical requirements for subcontractors and the like.
- Health and safety regulations (both federal and state).
- Municipal taxes for specific programs, such as schools or public transportation.
- Employee benefits such as insurance coverage (medical, dental, pre-paid legal), parking, retirement benefits, professional memberships, and so on.
- Union requirements, if you or your employees are subject to union contracts.
- Wage and hour laws (both federal and state). These include minimum wage and overtime requirements. In some states, the law also regulates holidays and vacations, as well as the method of paying employees during employment and upon termination.

As already noted, the requirements of these laws may vary dramatically from state to state, and craftspeople are well advised to discuss them with their lawyers, accountants, and bookkeepers. In addition, you should find out whether any other forms of employment legislation, such as licensing requirements, apply to you, your employees, or your business by consulting an attorney experienced in your type of business.

Termination of Employees

If the individual working for you is an independent contractor, the contract between you and that person will govern your respective rights regarding termination. On the other hand, if the individual is an employee, care must be taken not to become responsible for wrongful termination when dismissing the individual.

Historically, an employee who was not under contract could be terminated for any reason whatsoever. A number of years ago, this right of absolute dismissal was successfully challenged, and the rule was modified. At that time, it was held that an employee could be terminated for a right reason or for no reason at all, but not for a wrong reason. Thus, for instance, an employee who was terminated for refusing to commit perjury before a legislative committee was entitled to recover against the employer for wrongful termination. The public policy in having individuals testify honestly was considered more important than the employer's right to control the employment relationship.

Courts have become even more protective of the rights of employees. In a 1983 case, *Novosel v. Nationwide Insurance Company*, the United States Circuit Court of Appeals held that the power to hire and fire could not be used to dictate an employee's political activity, and that even a nongovernment entity is limited by the Constitution in its power to discharge an employee. The court, in essence, held that one's right to exercise constitutionally protected free speech was more important than the employer's right to control an employee's conduct.

Wrongful termination cases fall into at least four general categories. Employers may not legally terminate an employee for any of the following reasons:

1. Refusing to commit an unlawful act, such as perjury or participating in illegal price-fixing schemes
2. Performing a public obligation, such as serving on a jury or in a military reserve unit
3. Exercising a statutory right, such as filing a claim for workers' compensation or whistle-blowing
4. Discrimination

In a bizarre case, the Arizona Supreme Court held that an employee who was terminated for refusing to "moon" fellow employees in a parody of the song "Moon River" during a company retreat was entitled to damages for wrongful termination. The public policy of protecting her right of privacy was deemed more important than the employer's right to terminate an employee for insubordination.

The courts appear to go quite far in holding that an employer cannot discharge an employee without just cause. For instance, there are specific prohibitions on the termination of employees for "whistle-blowing," that is, notifying government authorities of wrongful acts by the employer, such as tax evasion or environmental pollution, or notifying corporate officers of wrongful acts of the employee's immediate supervisors.

An employer should have a legend in the employee handbook that makes it clear that the handbook is not an employment contract. Oral statements by interviewers might also be construed as imposing obligations on the employer. Employers often require prospective employees to sign a statement acknowledging that the employment is "at will" and does not give rise to any contractual rights.

If there is a probationary period after the hire, the employer should be careful to state that after the probationary period, the employee will become a "regular" or "full-time" employee, not a "permanent" employee. (If an employee is characterized as "permanent," then he or she may have a claim that the employer agreed never to terminate the employment contract.) In addition, any evaluation of the employee, either before or after the probationary period should be conducted fairly. When evaluations become merely pro forma, problems can and do arise. An employee may argue that he or she has received sparkling evaluations and is being terminated for an invalid reason.

To avoid misunderstanding or dispute, the employer should use what has been characterized as progressive discipline. The procedure begins with a verbal warning to an employee of your concern about a performance problem. If the problem persists, disciplinary practices are taken progressively until termination is the only recourse left. The entire process should be documented in the employee's file. Care should be taken to avoid implying that an employee will be reevaluated at the end of a specified period, since the employment might be terminated earlier. If you have an employee handbook, do not specify a disciplinary procedure unless you are prepared to strictly adhere to it.

When in doubt, an employer should contact an attorney with some experience in the field of employment relations. In this area, as with many others, seeking counsel before a problem occurs can prevent a good deal of time-consuming and costly litigation.

EMPLOYEE OR INDEPENDENT CONTRACTOR?

The following guidelines may be used when a question arises as to whether an individual is an employee or an independent contractor. It must be emphasized that if an employer-employee relationship exists, special contracts defining the relationship will not alter the fact that the individual is an employee. The following questions may help determine a person's status:

• Does the employer have the ability or right to hire, fire, set working hours, and control the individual's work? (Whether this right is exercised or not makes no difference. The key element in determining whether a person is an employee is the employer's ultimate right of control over the manner by which the work is done.)

- Does the employer or employee supply materials, supplies, or equipment? (An independent contractor is more likely to have his or her own tools and supplies.)
- How are expenses paid and records kept? (It is more likely that independent contractors would keep their own records, pay their own expenses, and be paid for a complete job rather than on an hourly basis.)
- What is the custom in the industry?
- What recourse does the employer have if the work is not done properly? (If an independent contractor is involved, the employer may refuse to pay for the entire job, while employees can be fired.)

An individual is more likely to be considered an independent contractor if the following criteria are met:

- The person is available to perform similar work for other individuals
- The person has a federal employer I.D. number ("EIN")
- The person is registered with an appropriate government agency, such as a licensing board
- The person is ultimately responsible to the purchaser if work is not properly done
- The person performs his or her own bookkeeping, insurance, advertising, etc.
- The person files appropriate tax returns as an independent contractor

This list is not all-inclusive, and a certain amount of judgment must be exercised in determining whether an individual is an employee or independent contractor. If there is any doubt about an individual's status, you should check with your attorney, since the characterization of his or her employment status can be crucial in determining whether you are responsible for such things as income tax withholding, employee benefits, workers' compensation, and the like.

HAZARDS IN THE WORKPLACE

On February 10, 1983, a sixty-one-year-old Polish-born employee of a film-recovery company in Chicago died of cyanide poisoning. He had worked for a small company that extracted silver from X-ray and photographic film. The work force consisted primarily of Polish immigrants and Mexican-American employees who spoke little English.

To extract the silver, the film-recovery workers put the film in a vat containing cyanide and then transferred the film to a second vat, which extracted the silver. The work was labor-intensive, and the vats were not properly vented and emitted dangerous fumes. Many of the employees complained of symptoms associated with cyanide poisoning, such as dizziness, nausea, and a bitter taste in the mouth. The employer made no efforts to warn them of the hazards of the work.

After the employee died and was examined by a county medical officer, it was determined that the cause of death was cyanide poisoning. Government officials examined the plant where the employee had worked and found numerous health and safety violations. Eight months later, the president of the company and numerous corporate officials, as well as the company itself, were charged with and convicted of murder. The court concluded that the company, its officers, and directors were aware of the serious risk and hazards resulting from cyanide use, but took no steps to alleviate the hazards in the plant. They did not even post warning signs that the foreign-born employees could understand.

While few manufacturers would intentionally injure a fellow human being, you may, nevertheless, find yourself in a similar situation. It is not uncommon to use toxic materials in craftsmaking. Often, employees are not aware of the potential hazard that may result from toxic materials.

It is advisable to research the potentially toxic effects of all substances used in your process or product, whether they are labeled for toxicity or not. You should then disclose pertinent information regarding hazardous substances to your employees, as well as the proper methods for their use. The federal Occupational Safety and Health Administration (OSHA) requires manufacturers of hazardous materials to provide material safety data sheets (MSDS) disclosing important information with respect to the proper use of such materials. These sheets should be maintained in the workplace and made available to employees. For more information about this subject, see *www.osha.gov/SLTC/hazardcommunications/index.html.*

Congress and federal administrative agencies are becoming more active in the regulation of hazardous substances. You should also be aware that your state workers' compensation agency or OSHA may have passed special rules regarding specific workplace substances and activities. It is critical to obtain a lawyer's opinion as to whether any of these regulations apply to your particular manufacturing process or other business. Your state's labor department may also be able to give you information regarding applicable workplace regulations.

Many manufacturers of art and crafts supplies have begun to voluntarily label their materials with health and safety warnings. Responding to pressure from arts-and-crafts advocate groups in 1979, Congress even considered a federal law entitled the Federal Art Hazard Bill. After shuttling through several committees, however, it died.

Following the pattern established by the federal lobbyists, several states, including California and Oregon, have enacted state arts-and-crafts labeling laws. Advocates of a healthy workplace are actively lobbying for similar laws throughout the United States.

An employer should advise new hires of all known hazards that may result from the work, and disclose the fact that there may be other undiscovered risks in using the particular materials involved in creating the craft. If an employment contract is used, a paragraph containing such a disclosure and the employee's acknowledgment of the known risks should be incorporated. A similar statement should also be included in any employment handbook.

While these documents would not provide a defense to a workers' compensation claim, they would sensitize employees to the need for caution in working with the toxic materials. Needless to say, you should take all precautions possible to protect the health and safety of your employees.

HOW TO FIND
A LAWYER

"*I want to see a lawyer!*"

That plaintive cry is heard most often when someone gets into a peck of trouble. But most lawyers are not Perry Masons, keeping people out of jail by dint of clairvoyant detective work and a facile court-room oration. Most people, fortunately, do not need lawyers for so serious a purpose. It is a rare individual, however, who gets through an entire life-time without needing a lawyer. A lawyer, like a doctor, is as essential in *preventing* problems before they arise as in solving them afterward.

Like doctors or craftspeople, lawyers specialize. Because the law has become so diverse and intricate, some lawyers handle only corporate law, others specialize in divorce, still others take only criminal cases, and so forth. Yet, there are still thousands of "general practitioners" who are well versed in the normal, ordinary problems most of us face: buying or selling a house, making a will, signing a contract, setting up a business venture. Of course, you do not need legal advice every time you sign something. A contract for a booth at a crafts fair, for example, is rarely worth the expense of a legal consultation.

WHEN TO GET A LAWYER

The New York State Bar Association provides this rule of thumb: "Get a lawyer's advice whenever you run into serious problems concerning your freedom, your financial situation, your domestic affairs, or your property." "Serious" is the important word in that sentence.

Legal matters fall into two basic classifications: civil and criminal.

Civil cases involve disputes between two parties, such as breach of contract, nonperformance of an obligation and the like, or an administrative action. A lawyer is necessary in such cases to protect your rights. In your business and personal affairs, a *transactional* lawyer can help to prevent complications that could cause you to end up in court in *civil litigation.*

Most small businesses would operate more efficiently and profitably in the long run if they had an ongoing relationship that allowed the attorney to get to know the business well enough to engage in preventive legal counseling. Legal problems almost always cost more to solve after they arise than it would have cost to prevent their occurrence.

Criminal cases concern violations of the criminal law, such as tax evasion, violation of environmental laws, and the like. In such cases, the government accuses a person of committing a specific crime. Under our legal system, it is presumed that a person is innocent until proven guilty. Every criminal defendant is entitled to a lawyer, even if the government has to pay the lawyer's fees because the defendant does not have the resources to hire a lawyer.

If you are ever confronted with a criminal matter that could lead to loss of liberty or property, the first call you should make is to a lawyer. Do not ever plead guilty to anything (except, perhaps, a parking ticket) without consulting a lawyer first. What may seem insignificant to you could well lead to serious consequences if you do not have proper legal advice.

The better part of wisdom is to have a lawyer before you need one. Sooner or later, you will probably need one.

WHERE TO FIND A LAWYER

Where do you find a good lawyer?

Since all lawyers are licensed, it is a matter of finding someone in whom you can have confidence, much as you would find a doctor or any other professional you trust. Ask friends or business acquaintances to recommend someone they have found to be satisfactory. You may want to talk to several lawyers before you settle on someone with whom you can establish that special relationship of confidence. Your state or local bar association may be able to recommend someone if you have a problem that requires specialized legal experience.

You can obtain more information about a lawyer by consulting the *Martindale-Hubbell Law Directory* in your local law library or at *www.martindale.com*, although, since there is a charge for the listing, not all lawyers are included in this directory. You may also wish to search the

World Wide Web. Most attorneys have established Web sites, and the better sites usually include résumés on the firm's attorneys. If your resources are very limited, the Legal Aid Society (or its local equivalent in your area) may be of help.

For information and possibly free legal services on problems related specifically to your work as a craftsperson, contact Volunteer Lawyers for the Arts, which has chapters in many states. See appendix A for a list of chapters.

DISCUSS FEES

When discussing a case with a lawyer, do not hesitate to discuss the fee. Fees usually depend upon the amount of time and research involved in the case, since business lawyers generally charge by the hour. With simple matters, an approximate fee can easily be determined, since your lawyer will have an idea of how much time will likely be necessary. For more complicated cases, you may only be given a general idea of the possible cost.

Some cases, especially lawsuits involving the recovery of money in accident cases, are often handled on a *contingency fee* basis. This means the lawyer gets a percentage of the recovery if the case is won, but gets nothing if the case is lost. Even in a lost case, however, the court costs and other out-of-pocket expenses have to be paid to the attorney by the client.

CONFIDENTIALITY

The relations between a lawyer and a client are, by law, confidential. A lawyer cannot be compelled—and, indeed, is not permitted—to reveal what has been discussed with a client without the client's permission. You should realize, however, that this confidential relationship exists to enable the lawyer to get all the information necessary, even such information as may be unfavorable to the client. A client's full and honest disclosure is the only way the lawyer can properly prepare a case and represent the client.

APPENDIX A:
VOLUNTEER LAWYER
ORGANIZATIONS

This information was updated using the Volunteer Lawyers for the Arts National Directory (*www.vlany.org*).

ARIZONA
Sam Sutton, Director
Cahill, Sutton & Thomas
2141 East Highland Avenue,
   #155
Phoenix, Arizona 85016
Tel: (602) 956-7000

CALIFORNIA
California Lawyers for the Arts
   (CLA)—San Francisco
Fort Mason Center
Building C, Room 255
San Francisco, California 94123
Tel: (415) 775-7200
E-mail: *cla@calawyersforthearts.org*

California Lawyers for the Arts
   (CLA)—Los Angeles
1641 18th Street
Santa Monica, California 90404
Tel: (310) 998-5590
Fax: (310) 998-5594
E-mail: *usercla@aol.com*

California Lawyers for the Arts
   (CLA)—Oakland
1212 Broadway Street, Suite 834
Oakland, California 94612
Tel: (510) 444-6351
Fax: (510) 444-6325

California Lawyers for the Arts
   (CLA)—San Diego
Attn: Craddock Stropes
625 Broadway, Suite 735
San Diego, California 92101
E-mail: *cstropes@sdpal.com*
Web site: *www.sandiegoperforms.com/
   volunteer/lawyer_arts.html*

California Lawyers for the Arts
   (CLA)—Sacramento
926 J Street, Suite 811
Sacramento, California 95814
Tel: (916) 442-6210
Fax: (916) 442-6281
E-mail: *clasacto@aol.com*

Beverly Hills Bar Association
Barristers Committee for the Arts
300 South Beverly Drive, Suite 201
Beverly Hills, California 90212
Tel: (310) 553-6644

COLORADO
Colorado Lawyers for the Arts
   (CoLA)
Post Office Box 48148
Denver, Colorado 80204
Tel: (303) 722-7994
Fax: (303) 778-0203
E-mail: *info@coloradoartslawyers.org*
Web site: *www.coloradoartslawyers.org*

CONNECTICUT
Connecticut Commission on the Arts
(CTVLA)
One Financial Plaza
Hartford, Connecticut 06103
Tel: (860) 566-4770
Fax: (860) 256-2811
Web site: www.ctarts.org/vla.htm

DISTRICT OF COLUMBIA
Washington Area Lawyers
    for the Arts (WALA)
1300 I Street NW, Suite 700
Washington, DC 20005
Tel: (202) 289-4295
Fax: (202) 289-4985
Web site: www.thewala.org

FLORIDA
Florida Volunteer Lawyers
    for the Arts
1350 East Sunrise Boulevard
Fort Lauderdale, Florida 33304
Tel: (954) 462-9191 x 324
Fax: (954-462-9182
E-mail: vla@artserve.org
Web site: www.artserve.org

GEORGIA
Southeast Volunteer Lawyers
    for the Arts
c/o Bureau of Cultural Affairs
675 Ponce De Leon Avenue,
    5th Floor
Atlanta, Georgia 30308
Tel: (404) 873-3911
Fax: (404) 817-6827
E-mail: gla@glarts.org
Web site: www.glarts.org

ILLINOIS
Lawyers for the Creative Arts (LCA)
213 West Institute Place, Suite 401
Chicago, Illinois 60610
Tel: (312) 649-4111
Fax: (312) 944-2195
Web site: www.law-arts.org

KANSAS
Mid-America Arts Resources
c/o Susan J. Whitfield-Lungren, Esq.
Post Office Box 363
Lindsborg, Kansas 67456
Tel: (913) 227-2321
E-mail: swhitfield@ks-usa.net

KENTUCKY
Lexington Arts & Cultural Council
Arts Place
161 North Mill Street
Lexington, Kentucky 40507
Tel: (859) 255-2951
Fax: (859) 255-2787
Web site: www.lexarts.org

LOUISIANA
Louisiana Volunteer Lawyers
    for the Arts (LVLA)
225 Baronne Street, Suite 1712
New Orleans, Louisiana 70112
Tel: (504) 523-1465
Fax: (504) 529-2430
Web site:
    www.artscouncilofneworleans.org

MAINE
Maine Lawyers for the Arts
Contact: Terry Cloutier, Esq.
Tel: (207) 871-7033
E-mail: tcloutier@lambertcoffin.com

Maine Lawyer Referral & Information
    Service
Main State Bar Association
Tel: (800) 860-1460 (toll-free)
Tel: (207) 622-1460 (local)
Web site:
    www.mainebar.org/lawyer_need.asp

MARYLAND
Maryland Lawyers for the Arts
Contact: Charles Frank Morgan
901 Dulaney Valley Rd., Suite 400
Towson, Maryland 21204
Tel: (410) 938-8800
Fax: (410) 938-8806

MASSACHUSETTS
Volunteer Lawyers for the Arts of
    Massachusetts, Inc.
249 A Street, Studio 14
Boston, Massachusetts 02110
Tel: (617) 350-7600
Tel: (617) 350-7600 TTY
Fax: (617) 350-7610
E-mail: *mail@vlama.org*
Web site: *www.vlama.org*
*Application forms for assistance
    available on Web site

MICHIGAN
ArtServe Michigan
Volunteer Lawyers for the Arts
    & Culture
17515 West Nine Mile Rd., Suite 1025
Southfield, Michigan 48075–4426
Tel: (248) 557-8288 x14
Fax: (248) 557-8581
E-mail: *kdabbs@artservemichigan.org*
Web site:
    www.artservemichigan.org/docs/
    services_sub/art_law.html

MINNESOTA
Springboard for the Arts
Resources and Counseling
    for the Arts
308 Prince Street, Suite 270
St. Paul, Minnesota 55101
Tel: (651) 292-4381
Fax: (651) 292-4315
E-mail: *info@RC4Arts.org*
Web site: *www.springboardforthearts.org*

MISSOURI
St. Louis Volunteer Lawyers and
    Accountants for the Arts
    (SLVLAA)
6128 Delmar Boulevard
St. Louis, Missouri 63112
Tel: (314) 863-6930
Fax: (314) 863-6932
Web site: *www.vlaa.org*
*Must submit application for assistance,
    which is available on Web site

MONTANA
Montana Arts Council Postal
Post Office Box 202201
Helena, Montana 59620-2201
Street Address:
316 N. Park Avenue, Suite 252
Helena, Montana 59620
Tel: (406) 444-6430
Fax: (406) 444-6548
E-mail: *mac@state.mt.us*

NEW HAMPSHIRE
Lawyers for the Arts/
    NewHampshire
One Granite Place
Concord, New Hampshire 03301
Tel: (603) 224-8300
Fax: (603) 226-2963
E-mail: *arts@nhbca.com*
Web site: *www.nhbca.com/*
    lawyersforarts.php

NEW YORK
Albany/Schenectady League of
    Arts Inc. (ALA)
161 Washington Avenue
Albany, New York 12207
Tel: (518) 449-5380
E-mail: *aslainfo@aol.com*

Volunteer Lawyers for the Arts
    (VLA)
One East 53rd Street, 6th Floor
New York, New York 10022
Tel: (212) 319-2787
Fax: (212) 752-6575
E-mail: *vlany@vlany.org*
Web site: *www.vlany.org*

Arts Council in Buffalo and Erie
    County
700 Main Street
Buffalo, New York 14202
Tel: (716) 856-7520
Fax: (716) 856-7548
E-mail: *info@artscouncilbuffalo.org*

NORTH CAROLINA
North Carolina Volunteer Lawyers for
    the Arts, Inc. (NCVLA)
Post Office Box 26513
Raleigh, North Carolina 27611-6513
Tel: (775) 255-5286
Fax: (775) 255-5286
E-mail: *info@ncvla.org*
Web site: *www.ncvla.org*

OHIO
Volunteer Lawyers and Accountants
    for the Arts (VLAA)
c/o The Cleveland Bar Association
113 Saint Clair Avenue, Suite 100
Cleveland, Ohio 44114
Tel: (216) 696-3525

Toledo Volunteer Lawyers and
    Accountants for the Arts
c/o Arnold Gottlieb, Esq.
608 Madison Avenue, Suite 1523
Toledo, Ohio 43604
Tel: (419) 255-3344
Fax: (419) 255-1329

OKLAHOMA
Oklahoma Accountants and Lawyers
    for the Arts
c/o Eric King, Gable & Gotwals
One Leadership Square, 15th Floor
211 North Robinson Avenue
Oklahoma City, Oklahoma 73102
Tel: (405) 235-5500
Fax: (405) 235-2875
E-mail: *eking@gablelaw.com*

OREGON
Oregon Lawyers for the Arts /
    Northwest Lawyers for the Arts
c/o Kohel Haver, Haver & Associates
621 South West Morrison Street,
    Suite 1417
Portland, Oregon 97205
Tel: (503) 295-2787
E-mail: *artcop@aol.com*

PENNSYLVANIA
Philadelphia Volunteer Lawyers
    for the Arts (PVLA)
251 South 18th Street
Philadelphia, Pennsylvania 19103
Tel: (215) 545-3385
Fax: (215) 545-4939
E-mail: *info@pvla.org*
Web site: *www.pvla.org*

ProArts–Pittsburgh Volunteer Lawyers
    for the Arts
425 Sixth Avenue, Suite 1220
Pittsburgh, Pennsylvania 15219-1835
Tel: (412) 391-2060
Fax: (412) 394-4280
E-mail: *proarts@proarts-pittsburgh.org*
Web site:
    www.proarts-pittsburgh.org/vla.htm

RHODE ISLAND
Ocean State Lawyers for the Arts
    (OSLA)
Post Office Box 19
Saunderstown, Rhode Island 02874
Tel: (401) 789-5686
E-mail: *dspatt@artslaw.org*
Web site: *www.artslaw.org*

SOUTH DAKOTA
South Dakota Arts Council (SDAC)
800 Governors Drive
Pierre, South Dakota 57501-2294
Tel: (605) 773-3131
Tel: (800) 423-6665 (in-state toll free)
Fax: (605) 773-6962
E-mail: *sdac@state.sd.us*

TENNESSEE
Tennessee Arts Commission
Citizens Plaza Building
401 Charlotte Avenue
Nashville, Tennessee 37243-0780
Tel: (615) 741-1701 (Voice/TDD)
Fax: (615) 741-8559
Web site: *www.arts.state.tn.us*

TEXAS
Artists' Legal and Accounting
    Assistance–Austin (ALAA)
Post Office Box 2577
Austin, Texas 78751
Tel: (512) 476-4458
E-mail: *mpolar@bga.com*

Lawyers and Accountants of North
    Texas for the Arts (LANTA)
Post Office Box 2019
Cedar Hill, Texas 75106
Tel: (972) 291-9010

Texas Accountants and Lawyers for
    the Arts (TALA)
1540 Sul Ross Street
Houston, Texas 77006
Tel: (713) 526-4876 x 201
Tel: (800) 526-8252 (toll free)
Fax: (713) 526-1299
E-mail: *info@talarts.org*
Web site: *www.talarts.org*

UTAH
Utah Lawyers for the Arts (ULA)
Post Office Box 652
Salt Lake City, Utah 84110
Contact: Andrew Deiss
E-mail: *adeiss@jonewaldo.com*

VIRGINIA
Virginia Lawyers for the Arts
Contact: Susan Jennings
E-mail: *adeiss@joneswaldo.com*

WASHINGTON
Washington Lawyers for the Arts
    (WLA)
819 North 49th Street, #207
Seattle, Washington 98103
Tel: (206) 328-7053
Fax: (206) 545-4866
E-mail: *director@wa-artlaw.org*
Web site: *www.wa-artlaw.org*

INTERNATIONAL VOLUNTEER LAWYER GROUPS

AUSTRALIA
Art Law Centre of Australia
The Gunnery
43-51 Cowper Wharf Road
Woolloomooloo, Sydney
New South Wales 2011
Australia
Tel: (800) 221 457 (toll free within
    Australia)
Tel: (02) 9356 2566
Fax: (02) 9358 6475
Web site: *www.artslaw.com.au*

CANADA
Canadian Artists' Representation
    (CARFAC)
401 Richmond Street West, Suite 440
Toronto, Ontario M5V 3A8
Tel: (416) 340-8850
Tel: (877) 890-8850
Fax: (416) 340-7653
E-mail: *carfacontario@carfacontario.ca*

Canadian Artists' Representation
    (CARFAC)
2 Daly Avenue, Suite 250
Ottawa, Ontario K1N 6E2
Web site: *www.carfac.ca* (For list of
    regional contacts and affilitates:
    www.carfac.ca/english/eng_regions.html)

APPENDIX B:
GLOSSARY OF COMMON
LEGAL TERMS

Accelerated depreciation *or* **accelerated cost recovery.** A method of recovering, through tax deductions, your investment in business equipment, such as a car, machine or building. This method allows the taxpayer to take larger deductions in the earlier years of the life of an asset. For example, under straight-line depreciation, for a machine that costs $1,000 and is to be depreciated over ten years, you could deduct $100 per year. But with accelerated depreciation you might deduct $250 the first year, $200 the second year, $100 the third year and decreasing amounts thereafter. These figures are only examples, of course, and you should consult a CPA or tax attorney if, in fact, you are going to take accelerated depreciation.

Assign. *verb* To transfer one's contractual rights and obligations to another party. This usually requires that party's permission.

Assign *or* **assignee.** *noun* The person or business to whom an agreement is assigned.

Author. In copyright terms, the person who created a work or the employer for whom an employee created a work within the scope of employment.

Contingency fee. A payment that will occur only if a certain event occurs. Attorneys sometimes take lawsuits on a contingency-fee basis, which means they will not be paid unless they win a verdict or settle a suit in favor of the client. If they do not win or settle, they are not paid fees (though the client will still be responsible for paying costs).

Contingency waiver. The intentional relinquishment of a known right that someone is entitled to by contract. This phrase is common in contracts. If the party with whom you have signed a contract does not do something the contract requires, such as pay within thirty days, and you do not terminate the contract as you are entitled to do, this does not mean that you cannot terminate the contract the next time the party is late in paying.

Employee at will. An employee who has not been hired for a set length of time and can be let go or quit at any time.

Estoppel. A legal action that prevents someone from claiming a right that is detrimental to another person if the second person has relied upon the conduct of the first. For example, if a supplier says you do not need to pay your bill this month because he understands you are in a cash-flow crisis and then learns that you are paying some other bills with the money that was earmarked for him, the supplier may be estopped from immediately suing you for the amount due because you relied on his statement.

Execute. To perform the necessary formalities of a contract, such as signing and dating.

Exposure. A position in which you could be injured. For example, you could risk serious exposure by signing an agreement that requires you to produce a large number of glass paperweights within a short period of time. If you do not produce all the paperweights you promised, you have exposed yourself to a lawsuit for not delivering everything you promised.

Fair use. A privilege of someone other than the copyright owner to use copyrighted material in a reasonable manner without the consent of the copyright owner. This is a technical concept for which guidelines are set forth in Section 107 of the Copyright Revision Act of 1976. It is a fair use, for example, to make a home video copy of a copyrighted television program so long as the copy is used for noncommercial purposes.

Injunction. A court order to do or stop doing something. If someone is copying your copyrighted item, you can seek an injunction ordering that person to stop copying. An injunction is commonly granted when a legal remedy like financial damages is insufficient to solve the problem and compensate you for your losses.

Integration. The inclusion of one agreement into a later one. A contract for you to provide a gallery with a certain number of stained-glass pieces may integrate a prior agreement between you and the gallery regarding prices or warranties.

Intellectual property. Products of the mind, including patents, copyrights, trade secrets, trade dress, or any special ideas you have that are used in producing your product.

Investment tax credit. A federal tax incentive program to encourage businesses to invest in equipment by allowing a percentage of the purchase price to be subtracted from the business taxes due. This is not simply a deduction.

Letters patent. A document issued by the federal government granting a patent to the patent owner.

Negotiable instrument. A legal term for a promise to pay that meets specific conditions. It must: (1) be in writing and signed by the maker, (2) contain an unconditional promise, (3) state a set sum of money to be paid, (4) indicate that payment will be made on demand or at a specific time, (5) show that payment is to the bearer or to order, and (6) contain no other promise. A check is an example of a negotiable instrument.

Other good and valuable consideration. A common contractual term promising that you will be compensated not only in money. The other person might promise, for example, not to compete with you for a certain period of time or in a certain geographical area, or may give you the first chance to buy certain products.

Publish. To make something known to the general public by putting it into circulation or by making statements about it. In the copyright sense, this means to distribute copies to the public.

Pursuant. To proceed from and in accordance with. A contract might state, "Pursuant to our agreement, I will send you six photographs in the mail within the next week."

Recitals. Statements at the beginning of a contract or other agreement that explain the reasons for the transaction.

Representation. Statements of fact made to cause another person to enter into an agreement. If you state that a piece of pottery is ovenproof, you are representing that it can be used in an oven without breaking.

Secured party. Someone who holds a security interest, for example, a mortgage lender or a person who sells an automobile in an installment sale.

Security interest. An interest granted in collateral in order to secure a debt. A mortgage is a security interest in real estate, because if payments are not made, the holder of the mortgage can enforce the security interest by selling the property to recover the amount of the loan.

Severability. Capable of being divided. If a contract has a severability clause and part of the contract is found to be void or illegal, the void or illegal parts may be taken out without necessarily destroying the rest of the contract.

Statute of limitations. A rule that prohibits bringing an action after a certain period of time has passed.

Title. Ownership. If you hold title to your car, house, or a work of art, it means you own it and can transfer it to someone else.

Trade dress. The distinctive "look and feel" of an item. The look and feel must be nonfunctional. For example, packaging, distinctive jewelry, and the distinctive overall theme (look and feel) of a fast-food restaurant could all be protectable.

Uniform Commercial Code (UCC). A uniform series of laws governing commercial transactions (sales of goods and negotiable instruments, secured transactions, and other commercial transactions) that has been adopted in all states (except Louisiana, which has adopted all but one section of the UCC).

Work of authorship. See Author.

APPENDIX C:
STANDARD LEGAL FORMS

Certificate of Authenticity
Disclosure Statement

Artist: _____

Title: _____

Medium: _____

Year of Production: _____

Medium of Original Work: _____

Year Original Work Was Created: _____

□ **This Multiple IS NOT Part of a Limited Edition**
□ **This Multiple IS Part of a Limited Edition**

This Multiple is Designated _____ of _____.

EDITION BREAKDOWN:

Name of Edition: _____

Number of Pieces Signed and Numbered: _____

Number of Pieces Signed Only: _____

Number of Pieces Numbered Only: _____

Description (if signed, method of signing): _____

EDITION SIZE:

The total edition size or number of Multiples with this Edition is _____ .

SIGNATURE:
Signed on Multiple by Artist and Numbered: _____
Signed on Master by Artist: _____
Stamped on Multiple by: _____
Stamped Only on Master by: _____

PRINTED OR PRODUCED BY:
_____
_____
_____
_____

ARTIST APPROVED, IN WRITING:
  ☐ The Master or Proofs Therefrom
  ☐ The Techniques Utilized in Production of This Multiple
  ☐ This Multiple and Its Production

[THIS MULTIPLE WAS:
  ☐ Handpulled
  ☐ Produced by Mechanical Means
  ☐ Produced by Photomechanical Means
  ☐ Produced by Photographic Means
  ☐ Produced by Other Means: _____]

PREVIOUS USE OF IMAGE:
This image ☐ was ☐ was not produced previously by a different process or medium or utilizing different paper, colors or color schemes. The total number of Multiples in [that] [those] previous edition[s] was _____ and was produced by _____
_____ on
_____ .

Description of Other Edition[s]: _____
_____

DISPOSITION OF MASTER:[1]
After [this] [these] Other Edition(s) [was] [were] produced, the Master was:
  ☐ Destroyed   ☐ Altered
  ☐ Effaced   ☐ Defaced
  ☐ Cancelled

USE OF MASTER:

_____

_____

_____

Artist was living when the Master for this Multiple was created, and the Edition was created during the Artist's lifetime [□ and was authorized by the Artist]. The Master for this Multiple □ was □ was not used for a prior limited edition. The Master □ was □ was not created from or reproduced from another limited edition. The total number of Multiples, including proofs, for all editions made from or including this Master is _____.

INVOLVEMENT OF ARTIST WITH PRINTER:
[□ The Artist her/himself] [□ A close associate of the Artist] inspected each phase of the printing process by _____ .

COMMENTS:

_____

_____

This image □ may □ shall not be reproduced again. [□ This image may have been or may in the future be used for other products, such as posters, promotional materials, gift items, etc.]

This Certificate of Authenticity accompanies all Multiples in this Edition.

_____   _____

Author's Signature   DATE

_____

[1]For graphics, the disposition of the plate(s) should be specified. Customarily, plates are canceled, i.e., defaced, after a limited edition is completed.

For sculptural works, the disposition of the mold(s) should be specified. Many artists break the mold(s) into as many pieces are there are in the edition and send one of these pieces to each owner of the editioned sculptures.

Commission Agreement

BETWEEN: Name   ("Purchaser")
                                      Address
                                      Phone Number
                                      Fax Number
                                      E-mail Address

AND: Name   ("Craftsperson")
                                      Address
                                      Phone Number
                                      Fax Number
                                      E-mail Address

Recitals

WHEREAS, Purchaser desires to commission Craftsperson to create [a piece of artwork] (the "Work") in Craftsperson's style; and

WHEREAS, a description of the Work is set forth in Exhibit A, attached hereto and incorporated herein;

Agreement

NOW, THEREFORE, in consideration of the mutual covenants contained herein, the parties agree as follows:

1. PRELIMINARY DESIGN AND MOCK-UP

1.1 Craftsperson agrees to create a Preliminary Design for the Work in the form of [sketches, paintings, maquettes, or the like], for which design work Purchaser agrees to pay a nonrefundable minimum design fee of _____ dollars ($_____) upon execution of this Agreement.

1.2 Within _____ (_____) days after the signing of this Agreement, Craftsperson shall deliver the Preliminary Design to Purchaser.

1.3 Purchaser shall have _____ (_____) days within which to accept the Preliminary Design or request specific modifications in writing. If specific modifications are required, Purchaser agrees to pay Craftsperson _____ Dollars ($_____) per hour as a redesign fee; however, Craftsperson shall not be required to work in excess of _____ (_____) hours or to provide more than _____ (_____) redesigns. Failure to inform Craftsperson of approval or rejection of the Preliminary Design within thirty (30) days of the date presented or sent to Purchaser shall be deemed to be an acceptance of the last submitted Preliminary Design.

1.4 Within _____ (_____) days after receiving Purchaser's required modifications, Craftsperson shall deliver a revised Preliminary Design to Purchaser.

1.5 Upon approval of the Preliminary Design, Craftsperson shall create working drawings showing placement of the Work and a Mock-Up of the installation for client approval. Purchaser shall have _____ (_____) days within which to accept the placement arrangement and Mock-Up or request specific modifications in writing. If specific modifications are required, Purchaser agrees to pay Craftsperson _____ dollars ($_____) per hour as a redesign fee; however, Craftsperson shall not be required to work in excess of _____ (_____) hours or to provide more than _____ (_____) redesigns. Failure to inform Craftsperson of approval or rejection of the placement arrangement and Mock-Up within thirty (30) days of the date presented or sent to Purchaser shall be deemed to be an acceptance of the last submitted placement arrangement and Mock-Up.

1.6 Within _____ (_____) days after receiving Purchaser's required modifications, Craftsperson shall deliver revised placement drawings and/or Mock-Up to Purchaser.

1.7 All Preliminary Designs, Mock-Ups, and the like shall remain the property of Craftsperson.

2. PURCHASE PRICE AND SCHEDULE OF PAYMENTS

2.1 Purchaser agrees to pay the Purchase Price of _____ dollars ($_____) for construction and installation of the Work, which amount is over and above the fees set forth in Section 1 hereof, as follows:

2.1.1 One-third (⅓) upon approval of the Mock-Up;

2.1.2 One-third (⅓) upon Craftsperson giving written notification to Purchaser that one-half (½) of the Work is completed;

2.1.3 The balance upon Craftsperson giving written notification to Purchaser that the Work is completed and prior to shipment of the Work to the installation site.

2.2 In addition, Purchaser shall pay all travel costs for Craftsperson to install the Work, including but not limited to airfare, lodging, and meals.

2.3 Purchaser agrees to pay all applicable sales taxes on the Work, if any, with the final payment.

2.4 If Purchaser fails to make any payment when due, Purchaser will be charged interest at the rate of one and one-half percent (1½%) per month (eighteen percent [18%] per annum) on amounts past due, and Craftsperson may cease work until payments are brought current.

2.5 Purchaser shall not unreasonably withhold acceptance of or payment for the Work. Purchaser's objection to any feature of the Work not specifically indicated in the Preliminary Design or Mock-Up but attributable to the exercise of Craftsperson's professional judgment in the creation of the Work on the basis of the Preliminary Design or Mock-Up shall not justify Purchaser's withholding acceptance of or payment for the Work.

2.6 In the event Purchaser unreasonably rejects the Work, Purchaser shall pay Craftsperson such additional sums as will raise the total amount of payment for the Work to one hundred percent (100%) of the Purchase Price.

2.7 Title to the Work shall remain in Craftsperson until Craftsperson is paid in full.

3. INSTALLATION

3.1   Craftsperson agrees to use his/her/its best efforts to complete installation of the Work within _____ (____) months from the date of Purchaser's approval of the placement arrangement and Mock-Up.

3.2   If the completion of the Work is delayed by the acts or omissions of Purchaser, Purchaser's failure to make payments when due, labor disputes, fire, theft, shortages of materials, unusual transportation delays, or by natural calamities or other reasons outside of Craftsperson's control, Craftsperson shall be entitled to extend the completion date by written notification to Purchaser by a period of time equal to the period of such delay.

3.3   In the event of an incapacitating illness or injury to Craftsperson, Craftsperson shall be entitled to extend the completion date by written notification to Purchaser, by a period of time equal to the period Craftsperson was ill or injured.

3.4   Purchaser shall, at his/her/its expense, prepare the installation site for mounting of the Work and provide the equipment necessary or appropriate for installation of the Work.

3.5   Purchaser shall, at his/her/its expense, have the Work shipped to the installation site.

3.6   Time shall not be considered of the essence with respect to the completion and installation of the Work.

3.7   At the time of installation, Craftsperson shall provide Purchaser with a lighting design for the Work unless otherwise specifically agreed in writing.

3.8   The Purchaser may, at reasonable times and subject to Craftsperson's availability, review the Work in progress. Such visits shall be preceded by written notification to the Craftsperson _____ (____) days prior to such visit. If, prior to the Work's completion, the Purchaser observes or otherwise becomes aware of any fault or defect in the work or nonconformance with the preliminary design, s/he/it shall promptly notify the Craftsperson in writing.

4. TERMINATION

This Agreement may be terminated under the following circumstances:

4.1   Purchaser does not approve the Preliminary Design, placement arrangement, or Mock-Up pursuant to Section 1. In such event, Craftsperson shall keep all payments and the Preliminary Design, placement arrangement, and/or Mock-Up created pursuant to that section.

4.2   Craftsperson shall have the right to terminate this Agreement if, pursuant to Section 2, Purchaser is late in making any payment. Notwithstanding anything to the contrary herein, Craftsperson shall be entitled to all other remedies provided at law or equity in the event of late or nonpayment.

4.3   The notification of the exercise of a right of termination under this section shall be in writing and shall set forth the grounds for termination.

4.4   Either party may terminate this Agreement upon written notice to the other party if the other party materially breaches this Agreement and such breach remains uncured for thirty (30) days following written notice of breach by the non-breaching party.

4.5   This Agreement shall terminate immediately and without any requirement of notice in the event that either party becomes insolvent, files a petition in bankruptcy, files a petition seeking any reorganization, arrangement, composition, or similar relief or proceeding under any applicable law regarding insolvency or relief for debtors, or makes an assignment for the benefit of creditors or similar undertaking, or if a receiver, trustee, or similar officer is appointed for all or a substantial portion of its business or assets.

4.6   Upon termination of this Agreement for any reason, all rights herein granted shall revert to Craftsperson. Purchaser shall return to Craftsperson all Preliminary Designs, Mock-Ups and other incidental works made in the creation of the Work, all copies and reproductions thereof and of the Work itself, and the Work.

5. ENGINEERS AND ARCHITECTS
Craftsperson agrees to work with Purchaser's engineers and architects as is reasonably necessary for completion and installation of the Work.

6. INTELLECTUAL PROPERTY RIGHTS
6.1   Craftsperson reserves all intellectual property rights, including but not limited to copyright and trade dress, in the Work, the Preliminary Design, Mock-Up, and any other incidental works made in the creation of the Work.

6.2   Craftsperson shall be entitled to customary and appropriate identification as the creator of the Work, including, where appropriate, publication of Craftsperson's copyright notice as follows: © by [Name], [Date]

7. NONDESTRUCTION, ALTERATION AND MAINTENANCE
7.1   Purchaser shall, at his/her/its expense, install and maintain lighting for the Work, as set forth in the design provided to Purchaser by Craftsperson, and shall maintain the Work, following all instructions provided Purchaser by Craftsperson.

7.2   Purchaser agrees to not intentionally or negligently destroy, damage, alter, modify, or otherwise change the Work in any way whatsoever.

7.3   If any alteration of any kind occurs to the Work after receipt by Purchaser, whether intentional or otherwise and whether done by Purchaser or others, Purchaser shall notify Craftsperson in writing, and Craftsperson has the right to request that the Work shall no longer be represented to be the work of Craftsperson.

7.4   Purchaser shall notify Craftsperson promptly in writing in the event of the need for any maintenance or restoration services so that Craftsperson shall have a reasonable opportunity either to perform such work itself or to supervise or consult in its performance. Craftsperson shall be reasonably compensated by Purchaser at a rate which reflects the current fair market value of such work, plus the cost of any materials, transportation, necessary equipment, or the like, for all such maintenance or restoration services.

7.5 In the event of possible alteration or destruction of the Work due to proposed renovation or demolition of a structure to or in which the Work is affixed, Craftsperson shall be entitled to written notification by Purchaser, affording Craftsperson a reasonable opportunity to reclaim the Work by removing it whole at his/her/its own expense, provided, however, Craftsperson shall be responsible for repairing any damages to any structure other than the one to be renovated or destroyed occasioned by such removal.

7.6 This section shall survive termination or closure of this Agreement.

8. LIMITED WARRANTY AND LIABILITY

8.1 Craftsperson agrees to replace or repair any part of the Work defective in workmanship or materials for a period of one (1) year after the completion of the initial installation. After the termination of the warranty period, Purchaser shall hold Craftsperson harmless from and against any and all liability.

8.2 EXCEPT AS EXPRESSLY SET FORTH HEREIN, CRAFTSPERSON GRANTS NO OTHER WARRANTIES, EXPRESS OR IMPLIED, REGARDING THE WORK, AND CRAFTSPERSON SPECIFICALLY DISCLAIMS ANY IMPLIED WARRANTY OF MERCHANTABILITY OR FITNESS FOR A PARTICULAR PURPOSE. NO ORAL OR WRITTEN INFORMATION OR ADVICE GIVEN BY CRAFTSPERSON OR HER/HIS/ITS AGENTS SHALL CREATE A WARRANTY OR IN ANY WAY INCREASE THE SCOPE OF THE WARRANTIES CONTAINED IN THIS AGREEMENT, AND PURCHASER MAY NOT RELY ON ANY SUCH INFORMATION.

8.3 Craftsperson shall not be liable or deemed to be in default for any delay or failure of performance under this Agreement resulting directly or indirectly from acts of nature, civil or military authority, governmental acts, orders or restrictions, acts of a public enemy, war, riots, civil disturbances, accidents, fire, explosions, earthquakes, floods, the elements, strikes, lockouts, labor disturbances, shortages of suitable parts, labor or transportation, delays caused by suppliers, or any other cause beyond the reasonable control of such party.

8.4 This section shall survive termination or closure of this Agreement.

9. RESALE ROYALTY

If Purchaser sells the Work or exchanges or barters it for another Work, Purchaser agrees to pay the Craftsperson ten percent (10%) of either the excess of the gross amount realized from the sale of the Work over the purchase price or the fair market value of the Work received in exchange or in barter over the purchase price.

10. MISCELLANEOUS

10.1 This Agreement or the rights, responsibilities, or obligations granted or assumed in this Agreement may not be assigned by either party hereunder, in whole or in part.

10.2 All notices required by this Agreement shall be made in writing, postage prepaid, certified mail, return receipt requested, or by facsimile transmission to the addresses or numbers first given above, or by e-mail to the address first given above, or by hand delivery. Notice shall be deemed received two (2) days after the date of mailing or the day after it is faxed, e-mailed, or hand delivered.

10.3   In the event that action, suit, or legal proceedings are initiated or brought to enforce any or all of the provisions of this Agreement, the prevailing party shall be entitled to such attorney fees, costs, and disbursements as are deemed reasonable and proper by an arbitrator or court. In the event of an appeal of an initial decision of an arbitrator or court, the prevailing party shall be entitled to such attorney fees, costs, and disbursements as are deemed reasonable and proper by the appellate court(s).

10.4   In the event it becomes necessary for Craftsperson to turn Purchaser's account over to an attorney or collection agency, Craftsperson shall be entitled to recover from Purchaser, and Purchaser expressly agrees to pay, all costs incurred by Craftsperson related to such collection activities, whether or not any suit, action, or other legal proceeding is instituted, and including but not limited to attorney fees, costs, and expenses, at arbitration, trial, or on appeal.

10.5   This Agreement shall be deemed executed in the State of [*State Where You Reside*] and shall be interpreted and construed in accordance with the laws of the State of [*State Where You Reside*] relating to contracts made and performed therein. Venue shall be proper only in the County of [*County Where You Reside*], State of [*State Where You Reside*].

10.6   This Agreement constitutes the entire Agreement between the parties and supersedes all prior agreements, understandings, and proposals (whether written or oral) in respect to the matters specified.

10.7   No alteration, modification, amendment, addition, deletion, or change to this Agreement shall be effective or binding unless and until such alterations, modifications, amendments, additions, deletions, or changes are properly executed in writing by both parties.

10.8   All headings used in this Agreement are for reference purposes only and are not intended or deemed to limit or affect, in any way, the meaning or interpretation of any of the terms and provisions of this Agreement.

10.9   It is expressly agreed by the parties hereto that the judicial rule of construction that a document should be more strictly construed against the draftsman thereof shall not apply to any provision.

10.10   No waiver by either party of any breach or default hereunder shall be deemed a waiver of any repetition of such breach or default or in any way affect any of the other terms and conditions hereof.

10.11   If any provision of this Agreement is judicially declared to be invalid, unenforceable, or void by a court of competent jurisdiction, such decision shall not have the effect of invalidating or voiding the remainder of this Agreement, and the part(s) of this Agreement so held to be invalid, unenforceable or void shall be deemed stricken, and the Agreement will be reformed to replace such stricken provision with a valid and enforceable provision which comes as close as possible to expressing the intention of the stricken provision. The remainder of this

Agreement shall have the same force and effect as if such part or parts had never been included.

10.12 This Agreement is effective as of the date all parties hereto have executed this Agreement.

10.13 This Agreement may be executed in two (2) or more counterparts, each of which shall be deemed an original, but all of which together shall constitute one and the same Agreement.

PURCHASER
[Purchaser's Name]

By: _____   _____

　　　Name: [Owner or Owner's Representative]　　　DATE
　　　Its: [Title]

CRAFTSPERSON
[Your Business Name]

By: _____   _____

　　　Name: [You or Your Representative]　　　DATE
　　　Its: [Title]

EXHIBIT A

Description of the Work:

Approximate Size of the Work:

Materials and Construction Method to Be Used:

Gallery Consignment Agreement

BETWEEN: Name   ("Craftsperson")
                            Address
                            Phone Number
                            Fax Number
                            E-mail Address

AND: Name   ("Gallery")
                            Address
                            Phone Number
                            Fax Number
                            E-mail Address

Recital

WHEREAS, Gallery wishes to sell Craftsperson's work (the "Artwork") on consignment;

Agreement

NOW, THEREFORE, in consideration of the mutual covenants contained herein, the parties agree as follows:

1. Consignment. Craftsperson hereby consigns to Gallery, subject to the terms of this Agreement, the Artwork listed on the initial, signed Inventory Sheet attached hereto as Exhibit A and incorporated herein. Additional Inventory Sheets may be incorporated into this Agreement if both parties agree to consignment of additional works by signing such additional Inventory Sheets in duplicate.

2. Duration of Consignment. Craftsperson and Gallery agree that the initial term of consignment for each piece of Artwork is to be _____ (____) months. Thereafter, consignment shall continue until this Agreement is terminated pursuant to Section 14 hereof.

3. Representations and Warranties of Craftsperson. Craftsperson hereby represents and warrants to Gallery that, to the best of her/his knowledge, s/he is the creator of the Artwork; s/he is the sole and exclusive owner of all rights granted to Gallery in this Agreement, and has not assigned, pledged, or otherwise encumbered the same; the Artwork is original; s/he has the full power to enter into this Agreement and to make the grants herein contained; and the Artwork does not, in whole or in part, infringe any copyright or violate any right to privacy or other personal or property right whatsoever, or contain any libelous matter or matter otherwise contrary to law.

4. Responsibility for Loss or Damage. For the purposes of any liability of Gallery, the value of the Artwork shall be the amount Craftsperson would receive if the Artwork had been sold.

5. Pricing, Gallery's Commission, and Terms of Payment.

5.1 Unless Craftsperson agrees otherwise in writing, Gallery shall sell Artwork only at the retail price specified on the Inventory Sheet(s). Gallery agrees not to sell Craftperson's Work on a layaway or installment basis without Craftsperson's prior written approval.

5.2 Gallery's commission shall be _____ percent (___%) and Craftsperson shall be paid the remaining _____ percent (___%) of the sales price of each piece of Artwork sold.

5.3 Payment to Craftsperson on all sales made by Gallery shall be within _____ (__) days after the date of sale of the Artwork and shall be accompanied by a copy of the sales receipt, which shall include the name and sales price of the Artwork and the name and address of the purchaser. On installment sales, all proceeds received on each installment shall be paid to Craftsperson until Craftsperson is paid in full. In the event that the Artwork is subsequently returned to Gallery for a refund, Craftsperson shall promptly return to Gallery any fee s/he received or, at Gallery's discretion, Gallery may deduct such amount from the next payment due Craftsperson.

5.4 Gallery may purchase any piece of Artwork at a price equal to the share of the sales price to which Craftsperson would be entitled if the sale had been made to a third party. Payment for any such purchase by Gallery shall be made to Craftsperson within _____ (__) days of such purchase.

6. Accounting.

6.1 Gallery shall maintain accurate books and records reflecting its gross sales and the amount due Craftsperson. Craftsperson, at her/his own expense, shall have the right to examine, during regular business hours and upon reasonable notice, Gallery's records which reflect payments due Craftsperson. In the event such an examination of Gallery's records results in the determination that the amount of payments was miscalculated and resulted in a deficiency, then the amount of the miscalculation, including interest at ten percent (10%) per annum and the cost of such examination (including all reasonable attorney and accounting fees incurred for such examination), shall be paid by Gallery to Craftsperson with the monthly statement following such examination.

6.2 With each payment made by Gallery to Craftsperson, but in any event no less than quarterly, a statement of accounts for all sales of Artwork shall be furnished by Gallery to Craftsperson. Craftsperson shall have the right to inventory her/his Artwork in Gallery's possession and to review, at Gallery's place of business, copies of records pertaining to sales of the Artwork. Gallery will assist Craftsperson, at no charge, with the inventory review. Any such review must be arranged for in advance by giving Gallery at least one (1) week's written notice.

7. Transportation Responsibilities.
Packing and shipping charges, insurance costs, other handling expenses, and risk of loss or damage incurred in the delivery of Artwork from Craftsperson to Gallery shall be borne by Craftsperson. Packing

and shipping charges, insurance costs, other handling expenses, including but not limited to transportation of Artwork while in Gallery custody, and risk of loss or damage incurred in the return of Artwork from Gallery to Craftsperson shall be the responsibility of and borne by Gallery.

8. Removal of Artwork. Gallery shall not be liable to Craftsperson for loss of or damage to a piece of Artwork if Craftsperson fails to remove the Artwork within a period of _____ (__) days following the date set forth herein for such removal or within a period of _____ (__) days after notice to remove the Artwork has been sent by certified mail to Craftsperson's last address known to Gallery. Failure to so remove a piece of Artwork shall terminate the trust relationship between Gallery and Craftsperson.

9. Return of Artwork. Craftsperson may request Gallery to return any piece of Artwork for which Gallery has not received an approved downpayment. Gallery shall, within _____ (__) days, return that Artwork to Craftsperson.

10. Title. Each piece of the Artwork is trust property in the hands of Gallery, which is a trustee for the benefit of Craftsperson until such Artwork is sold to a bona fide third party or, if the Artwork is bought by Gallery, until the full price is paid to Craftsperson. Upon any such sale, the proceeds of the sale (including any unpaid receivables) are trust property in the hands of Gallery, which is a trustee for the benefit of Craftsperson until the amount due Craftsperson from the sale has been paid to Craftsperson. Gallery agrees to execute any and all documents necessary to effectuate this Agreement, including but not limited to a UCC1 in favor of Craftsperson.

11. Promotion.
11.1 *Quality Control.* Gallery shall provide Craftsperson with samples of all literature, brochures, advertising, and the like which pertain to Craftsperson or Craftsperson's Artwork and shall obtain Craftsperson's written approval prior to using such materials.
11.2 *Best Efforts.* Gallery agrees to use its best efforts to promote, market, and sell the Artwork.

12. Reproduction. Craftsperson reserves all rights to the reproduction of Artwork, except as noted in writing to the contrary. Notwithstanding the foregoing, Craftsperson hereby agrees to permit Gallery to have Artwork photographed for any publicity or promotion of the exhibition of Artwork; provided that Gallery shall give Craftsperson a copy of every photograph or reproduction of Craftsperson's Artwork before it is used for publicity, and Craftsperson must approve such photographs or reproductions prior to their use. Gallery shall post a notice when Craftsperson's Artwork is displayed for sale that Artwork is copyrighted by Craftsperson and any unauthorized copying or photography of it is prohibited.

13. Insurance. Gallery shall, at its expense, insure all Artwork for at least sixty percent (60%) of its retail price and promptly provide Craftsperson with a copy of the insurance binder or policy covering the Artwork. Gallery shall name the Craftsperson as an insured under the policy, and, if Artwork is damaged or destroyed, Craftsperson shall receive the same amount as if Artwork had been sold.

14. Termination of Agreement. Notwithstanding any other provision of this Agreement, but subject to Section 4, this Agreement may be terminated at any time by either Gallery or Craftsperson by means of a thirty (30) day written notification of termination from either party to the other. In the event of Craftsperson's death, the estate of Craftsperson shall be considered to be Craftsperson for purposes of this Agreement. After the notification of termination has been received, Gallery and Craftsperson shall settle all accounts according to the usual process and time limits set forth in this Agreement.

15. Assignability. This Agreement or the rights, responsibilities, or obligations granted or assumed in this Agreement may not be assigned by either party hereto, in whole or in part.

16. Notices. All notices required by this Agreement shall be made in writing, postage prepaid, certified mail, return receipt requested, or by facsimile transmission to the addresses or numbers first given above, or by hand delivery. Notice shall be deemed received two (2) days after the date of mailing or the day after it is faxed, e-mailed, or hand delivered.

17. Attorney Fees. In the event that action, suit, or legal proceedings are initiated or brought to enforce any or all of the provisions of this Agreement, the prevailing party shall be entitled to such attorney fees, costs, and disbursements as are deemed reasonable and proper by an arbitrator or court. In the event of an appeal of an initial decision of an arbitrator or court, the prevailing party shall be entitled to such attorney fees, costs, and disbursements as are deemed reasonable and proper by the appellate court(s).

18. Venue. This Agreement shall be deemed executed in the State of [*State Where You Reside*] and shall be interpreted and construed in accordance with the laws of the State of [*State Where You Reside*] relating to contracts made and performed therein. Venue shall be proper only in the County of [*County Where You Reside*], State of [*State Where You Reside*].

19. Merger. This Agreement constitutes the entire agreement between the parties and supersedes all prior agreements, understandings, and proposals (whether written or oral) in respect to the matters specified.

20. Modification. No alteration, modification, amendment, addition, deletion, or change to this Agreement shall be effective or binding unless and until such alterations, modifications, amendments, additions, deletions, or changes are properly executed in writing by both parties.

21. Headings. All headings used in this Agreement are for reference purposes only and are not intended or deemed to limit or affect, in any way, the meaning or interpretation of any of the terms and provisions of this Agreement.

22. Judicial Rule of Construction. It is expressly agreed by the parties hereto that the judicial rule of construction that a document should be more strictly construed against the draftsman thereof shall not apply to any provision.

23. Waiver. No waiver by either party of any breach or default hereunder shall be deemed a waiver of any repetition of such breach or default or in any way affect any of the other terms and conditions hereof.

24. Severability. If any provision of this Agreement is judicially declared to be invalid, unenforceable, or void by a court of competent jurisdiction, such decision shall not have the effect of invalidating or voiding the remainder of this Agreement, and the part(s) of this Agreement so held to be invalid, unenforceable or void shall be deemed stricken, and the Agreement will be reformed to replace such stricken provision with a valid and enforceable provision which comes as close as possible to expressing the intention of the stricken provision. The remainder of this Agreement shall have the same force and effect as if such part or parts had never been included.

25. Effective Date. This Agreement is effective as of the date all parties hereto have executed this Agreement.

26. Counterparts. This Agreement may be executed in two (2) or more counterparts, each of which shall be deemed an original, but all of which together shall constitute one and the same Agreement.

CRAFTSPERSON

_____   _____

Name: [Your Name]   DATE
SSN: _____

GALLERY
[Gallery Name]

By: _____   _____

    Name: [Owner's Name or Representative]   DATE
    Its: [Title]
TIN: _____

EXHIBIT A

Name of Work:

Description:

Medium:

Retail Price:

Assignment of Copyright

BETWEEN: Name   ("Assignor")
                            Address
                            Phone Number
                            Fax Number
                            E-mail Address

AND: Name   ("Assignee")
                            Address
                            Phone Number
                            Fax Number
                            E-mail Address

1. Consideration and Assignment. In consideration of _____ dollars ($_____), receipt of which is hereby acknowledged, Assignor sells and assigns to Assignee all of her/his/its right, title, and interest in and to the work described on Exhibit A, attached hereto and incorporated herein (the "Work"), and the copyright therein, together with the right to secure renewals, reissues, and extensions of such copyright.[1] Assignor also sells, assigns, and transfers all of the claims and demands which Assignor might have against all persons who may have heretofore infringed any of the rights conveyed hereby.

2. Term. This Assignment shall extend to the full term remaining of the copyright and any applicable renewal or extension thereof.

3. Assignor's Representation and Warranties. Assignor hereby represents and warrants to Assignee, any seller or distributor of the Work, and any officers, agents and employees of the foregoing that, to the best of her/his/its knowledge:
    3.1   S/he/it is the creator of the Work;
    3.2   S/he/it warrants and represents that s/he/it is the sole owner of all rights in the Work, including but not limited to the copyright therein, and that s/he/it has federal statutory copyright protection in the Work, which copyright was registered with the United States Copyright Office on _____, and assigned the Certificate of Registration No. _____, and has not assigned, pledged, or otherwise encumbered the same;
    3.3   The Work is original and is not in the public domain;
    3.4   S/he/it has the full power to enter into this Agreement and to make the grants herein contained; and
    3.5   The Work does not, in whole or in part, infringe any copyright or violate any right to privacy or other personal or property right whatsoever, or contain any libelous matter or matter otherwise contrary to law.
    3.6   [In the event Assignee shall be rendered liable for any damages which result from Assignor's breach of the above representations and warranties, then Assignor agrees to hold Assignee harmless from and against such liability, including all reasonable attorney fees incurred on any trial or appeal.][2]

3.7 This section will survive the term of this Agreement for any reason.

4. Miscellaneous. This Agreement constitutes the entire agreement between the parties and supersedes all prior agreements, understandings and proposals (whether written or oral) in respect to the matters specified. No agreement or understanding that alters or extends the meaning of this contract shall be binding unless in writing and signed by the parties hereto. Any and all references to Paragraphs and/or Sections shall be deemed references to Paragraphs and/or Sections of this Agreement unless the context shall otherwise require. If any provision of this Agreement is judicially declared to be invalid, unenforceable or void by a court of competent jurisdiction, such decision shall not have the effect of invalidating or voiding the remainder of this Agreement, and the part(s) of this Agreement so held to be invalid, unenforceable or void shall be deemed stricken, and the Agreement will be reformed to replace such stricken provision with a valid and enforceable provision which comes as close as possible to expressing the intention of the stricken provision. The remainder of this Agreement shall have the same force and effect as if such part or parts had never been included. This Agreement is effective as of the date all parties hereto have executed this Agreement. This Agreement is deemed a contract made in [*State Where You Reside*], and it shall be construed and enforced according to the laws of the State of [*State Where You Reside*]. Any suit or action instituted by either party to enforce the terms shall be brought in the courts in the State of [*State Where You Reside*]. Venue is proper only in [*County Where You Reside*] County in [*State Where You Reside*]. In the event suit or action is instituted to enforce collection or any of the terms of this contract, the prevailing party shall be entitled to recover from the other party such sum as the court deems reasonable as attorney fees at arbitration, on trial or on appeal, in addition to all other sums provided by law.

ASSIGNOR

_____   _____

Name: [Your Name]   DATE

ASSIGNEE
[Business Name]

By: _____   _____

    Name: [Owner's Name or Representative]   DATE
    Its: [Title]

---

[1] There is no renewal in the United States for works created on or after January 1, 1978, although other countries may still have renewal periods.

[2] If you are the Assignor, you will probably not wish to include this "hold harmless" section in your contract. If you are the Assignee, you will want this liability protection.

Copyright Licensing Agreement

BETWEEN: Name   ("Licensor")
                                Address
                                Phone Number
                                Fax Number
                                E-mail Address

AND: Name   ("Licensee")
                                Address
                                Phone Number
                                Fax Number
                                E-mail Address

Recitals

WHEREAS, Licensor owns all intellectual property rights, including the copyrights, in and to the works set forth in Exhibit A, attached hereto and incorporated herein (the "Works"); and

WHEREAS, Licensee desires to reproduce, manufacture, distribute, promote, market, and/or sell the Works;

Agreement

NOW, THEREFORE, in consideration of the mutual covenants contained herein, the parties agree as follows:

1. License. Licensor grants to Licensee the right to manufacture, reproduce, distribute, promote, market, and/or sell the Works. This license shall be exclusive[1] and shall not be transferable without Licensor's prior written consent.

2. Representations and Warranties of Licensor. Licensor hereby represents and warrants to Licensee that to the best of Licensor's knowledge:

2.1   Licensor is the sole and exclusive owner of all rights granted to Licensee in this Agreement, and has not assigned, pledged or otherwise encumbered the same;

2.2   Licensor has the full power to enter into this Agreement and to make the grants herein contained;

2.3   The Works do not, in whole or in part, infringe any copyright or violate any right to privacy or other personal or property right whatsoever, or contain any libelous matter or matter otherwise contrary to law.

3. Indemnity. In the event Licensee is rendered liable for any damages which result from Licensor's breach of the above representations and warranties, then Licensor agrees to hold Licensee harmless from and against such liability, including all reasonable attorney fees incurred on any trial or appeal. In the event Licensor is rendered liable for any damages as a result of any act or omission by Licensee in reproducing, manufacturing, distributing, marketing, and/or selling the Works, then Licensee agrees to hold Licensor harmless from and against such liability, including all reasonable attorney fees incurred on any trial or appeal.

4. Registration. Licensee may, at its own expense, register the copyrights in the Works with the United States Copyright Office in the name of Licensor.[2]

5. Compensation. Licensee shall pay Licensor an amount equal to _____ percent (____%) of Licensee's gross receipts [from sale, license, or other distribution of the Works]. "Gross receipts" as used herein shall be defined to include money, property, or anything of value received, directly or indirectly, in whatever form and from whatever source, by Licensee or any affiliate or subsidiary of Licensee, less returns. In the event Licensee distributes any Works without charge, Licensee shall pay Licensor the amount Licensor would have received had Licensee been paid its customary charges. Licensee shall render to Licensor, within one (1) month after each calendar quarter, a written report stating Licensee's total gross receipts from sales of the Works for the prior calendar quarter and the total payment due Licensor for the prior calendar quarter. Each quarterly statement shall be accompanied by a payment to Licensor of all sums due Licensor for the prior calendar quarter. If any payment is not made in full when due, the unpaid balance shall bear interest at ____ percent (____%) per annum.

6. Accounting. Licensee shall maintain accurate books and records reflecting its gross sales and the amount due Licensor. Licensor, at its own expense, shall have the right to examine, during regular business hours and upon reasonable notice, Licensee's records which reflect payments due Licensor.[3]

7. Indemnity. Licensor assumes no liability to Licensee or to third parties with respect to the Works reproduced, manufactured, distributed, marketed, and/or sold by Licensee under the copyright, other than as expressly set forth herein, and Licensee shall indemnify Licensor against losses incurred to claims of third parties against Licensor involving sale of Licensee's Works.

8. Termination. Except as otherwise provided herein, this Agreement shall remain in full force and effect, but is terminable at the will of Licensor upon not less than thirty (30) days' written notice to Licensee. Notwithstanding anything herein to the contrary, if Licensee makes any assignment of assets or business for the benefit of creditors, or a trustee or receiver is appointed to conduct its business or affairs, or it is adjudged in any legal proceeding to be either a voluntary or involuntary bankruptcy, then the rights granted herein shall forthwith cease and terminate without prior notice or legal action by Licensor. In the event of termination, all rights herein granted shall revert to Licensor, and Licensee agrees to assign any registration of the copyright to Licensor.

9. Ownership of Copyright. Licensee acknowledges Licensor's exclusive right, title, and interest in and to the copyright and any registration that has issued or may issue thereon, and will not at any time do or cause to be done any act or thing contesting or in any way impairing or tending to impair part of such right, title, and interest. Except as otherwise permitted herein, Licensee shall not in any manner represent that it has any ownership in the copyright or registrations thereof, and acknowledges that use of the copyright shall enure to the benefit of Licensor. On termination of this Agreement in any manner, Licensee will cease and desist from all use of the copyright in any way and will deliver up to Licensor, or its duly authorized representatives, all material and papers upon which the copyright appears, and furthermore, Licensee will not at any time adopt or use without Licensor's prior written consent, any work which is likely to be substantially or confusingly similar to the Work.

10. Miscellaneous. This Agreement constitutes the entire agreement between the parties and supersedes all prior agreements, understandings and proposals (whether written or oral) in respect to the matters specified. No agreement or understanding that alters or extends the meaning of this contract shall be binding unless in writing and signed by the parties hereto. Any and all references to Paragraphs and/or Sections shall be deemed references to Paragraphs and/or Sections of this Agreement unless the context shall otherwise require. If any provision of this Agreement is judicially declared to be invalid, unenforceable or void by a court of competent jurisdiction, such decision shall not have the effect of invalidating or voiding the remainder of this Agreement, and the part(s) of this Agreement so held to be invalid, unenforceable or void shall be deemed stricken, and the Agreement will be reformed to replace such stricken provision with a valid and enforceable provision which comes as close as possible to expressing the intention of the stricken provision. The remainder of this Agreement shall have the same force and effect as if such part or parts had never been included. This Agreement is effective as of the date all parties hereto have executed this Agreement. This Agreement is deemed a contract made in [State Where You Reside], and it shall be construed and enforced according to the laws of the State of [State Where You Reside]. Any suit or action instituted by either party to enforce the terms shall be brought in the courts in the State of [State Where You Reside]. Venue is proper only in [County Where You Reside] County in [State Where You Reside]. In the event suit or action is instituted to enforce collection or any of the terms of this contract, the prevailing party shall be entitled to recover from the other party such sum as the court deems reasonable as attorney fees at arbitration, on trial or on appeal, in addition to all other sums provided by law.

11. Counterparts. This Agreement may be executed in two (2) or more counterparts, each of which shall be deemed an original, but all of which together shall constitute one and the same Agreement.

LICENSOR
[Business Name]

By: _____   _____

    Name: [You or Your Representative]   DATE
    Its: [Title]

LICENSEE

_____   _____

Name: [Licensee's Name]   DATE

---

[1] If the license is to be nonexclusive, or if the Licensor desires to reserve any rights, this should be specified.

[2] If the Licensor has registered the Work with the Copyright Office, then you should state that "Licensor has federal statutory copyright protection in the Work, which copyright was registered with the United States Copyright Office on _____, and assigned the Certificate of Registration No. _____, and has not assigned, pledged, or otherwise encumbered the same."

[3] If you are the Licensor, you may wish to have the following language inserted here: In the event such an examination of Licensee's records results in the determination that the amount of payments was miscalculated, then the amount of the miscalculation, including interest at ten percent (10%) per annum and the cost of such examination (including all reasonable attorney's and accounting fees incurred for such examination), shall be paid by Licensee to Licensor in the quarterly statement following such examination.

Trademark Licensing Agreement

BETWEEN: Name   ("Licensor")
                           Address
                           Phone Number
                           Fax Number
                           E-mail Address

AND: Name   ("Licensee")
                           Address
                           Phone Number
                           Fax Number
                           E-mail Address

Recitals

WHEREAS, Licensor has adopted and is using the mark set forth in Exhibit A, attached hereto and incorporated herein, as a trademark for _____ _____ (the "Products") in the State of [*State Where You Reside*] and elsewhere in the United States or in any other country party to the Madrid Trademark Treaty (hereinafter "Trademark"); and;

WHEREAS, Licensee is desirous of using said Trademark for _____ _____ in the Territory;

Agreement

NOW, THEREFORE, in consideration of the mutual covenants contained herein, the parties agree as follows:

1. License. Licensor grants to Licensee the right to use under the common law and under the auspices and privileges provided by any registrations covering the same during the term of this Agreement, and Licensee hereby undertakes to use the Trademark in the Territory in connection with the sale of the Products.

2. Quality of Services. Licensee shall use the Trademark only with the Products in accordance with the guidance and directions furnished to Licensee by Licensor, or its representatives or agents, from time to time, if any, but always the quality of the Products shall be satisfactory to Licensor or as specified by it. Licensor shall be the sole judge of whether or not Licensee has met or is meeting the standards of quality so established.

3. Inspection. Licensee will permit duly authorized representatives of Licensor to inspect the premises of Licensee at all reasonable times, for the purpose of ascertaining or determining compliance with Paragraphs 1 and 2 hereof.[1]

4. Use of Trademark. Licensee shall provide Licensor with samples of all literature, brochures, signs, and advertising material prepared by Licensee, and Licensee shall obtain the approval of Licensor with respect to all such brochures, signs, and advertising material bearing the Trademark prior to the use thereof. When using the Trademark under this Agreement, Licensee undertakes to comply substantially with all laws pertaining to trademarks in force at any time in the Territory. This provision includes compliance with marking requirements.[1]

5. Registration. Licensee may, at its own expense, apply for registration of the Trademark in the name of Licensor on the United States Federal Register or in any country signatory to the Madrid Trademark Treaty.

6. Extent of License. The right granted in Paragraph 1 hereof shall be exclusive and shall not be transferable without Licensor's prior written consent.

7. Compensation. Licensee shall pay Licensor an amount equal to _____ _____ percent (____%) of Licensee's gross receipts [from the sale, license, or other distribution of the Products]. "Gross receipts" as used herein shall be defined to include money, property, or anything of value received, directly or indirectly, in whatever form and from whatever source, by Licensee or any affiliate or subsidiary of Licensee, less returns. In the event Licensee distributes any Products without charge, Licensee shall pay Licensor the amount Licensor would have received had Licensee been paid its customary charges. Licensee shall render to Licensor, within three (3) months after each calendar quarter, a written report stating Licensee's total gross receipts for the prior calendar quarter and the total payment due Licensor for the prior calendar quarter. Each quarterly statement shall be accompanied by a payment to Licensor for all sums due Licensor for the prior calendar quarter. If any payment is not made in full when due, the unpaid balance shall bear interest at _____ percent (____%) per annum.

8. Accounting. Licensee shall maintain accurate books and records reflecting its gross sales and the amount due Licensor. Licensor, at its own expense, shall have the right to examine, during regular business hours and upon reasonable notice, Licensee's records which reflect payments due Licensor.[2]

9. Indemnity. Licensor assumes no liability to Licensee or to third parties with respect to the performance characteristics of the Products manufactured, marketed, and sold by Licensee under the Trademark, and Licensee shall indemnify Licensor against losses incurred to claims of third parties against Licensor involving sale of Licensee's Products.

10. Termination. Except as otherwise provided herein, this Agreement shall remain in full force and effect, but is terminable at the will of Licensor upon not less than thirty (30) days' written notice to Licensee. Notwithstanding anything herein to the contrary, if Licensee makes any assignment of assets or business for the benefit of creditors, or a trustee or receiver is appointed to conduct its business or affairs, or it is adjudged in any legal proceeding to be either a voluntary or involuntary bankruptcy, then the rights granted herein shall forthwith cease and terminate without prior notice or legal action by Licensor. In the event of termination, all rights herein granted shall revert to Licensor, and Licensee agrees to assign any registration of the Trademark to Licensor.

11. Ownership of Trademark. Licensee acknowledges Licensor's exclusive right, title and interest in and to the Trademark and any Registration that has issued or may issue thereon, and will not at any time do or cause to be done any act or thing contesting or in any way impairing or tending to impair part of such right, title, and interest. Except as otherwise permitted herein, Licensee shall not in any manner represent that it has any ownership in the Trademark or registrations thereof, and acknowledges that use of the Trademark shall enure to the benefit of Licensor. On termination of this Agreement in any manner, Licensee will immediately cease and desist from all use of the Trademark in any way and will deliver up to Licensor, or its duly authorized representatives, all material and papers upon which the Trademark appears, and furthermore, Licensee will not at any time adopt or use without Licensor's prior written consent, any word or mark which is likely to be substantially or confusingly similar to the Trademark.

12. Miscellaneous. This Agreement constitutes the entire agreement between the parties and supersedes all prior agreements, understandings and proposals (whether written or oral) in respect to the matters specified. No agreement or understanding that alters or extends the meaning of this contract shall be binding unless in writing and signed by the parties hereto. Any and all references to Paragraphs and/or Sections shall be deemed references to Paragraphs and/or Sections of this Agreement unless the context shall otherwise require. If any provision of this Agreement is judicially declared to be invalid, unenforceable or void by a court of competent jurisdiction, such decision shall not have the effect of invalidating or voiding the remainder of this Agreement, and the part(s) of this Agreement so held to be invalid, unenforceable or void shall be deemed stricken, and the Agreement will be reformed to replace such stricken provision with a valid and enforceable provision which comes as close as possible to expressing the intention of the stricken provision. The remainder of this Agreement shall have the same force and effect as if such part or parts had never been included. This Agreement is effective as of the date all parties hereto have executed this Agreement. This Agreement is deemed a contract made in [*State Where You Reside*], and it shall be construed and enforced according to the laws of the State of [*State Where You Reside*]. Any suit or action instituted by either party to enforce the terms shall be brought in the courts in the State of [*State Where You Reside*]. Venue is proper only in [*County Where You Reside*] County in [*State Where You Reside*]. In the event suit or action is instituted to enforce collection or any of the terms of this contract, the prevailing party shall be entitled to recover from the other party such sum as the court deems reasonable as attorney fees at arbitration, on trial or on appeal, in addition to all other sums provided by law.

13. Counterparts. This Agreement may be executed in two (2) or more counterparts, each of which shall be deemed an original, but all of which together shall constitute one and the same Agreement.

LICENSOR

_____   _____

Name: [Your Name]   DATE

LICENSEE
[Business Name]

By: _____   _____

    Name: [Owner or Owner's Representative]   DATE
    Its: [Title]

---

[1]As mentioned in Chapter 12, a reservation of the rights to inspect and approve of the use of the licensed mark is necessary in any trademark license.

[2]If you are the Licensor, you may wish to have the following language inserted here: In the event such an examination of Licensee's records results in the determination that the amount of payments was miscalculated, then the amount of the miscalculation, including interest at ten percent (10%) per annum and the cost of such examination (including all reasonable attorney's and accounting fees incurred for such examination), shall be paid by Licensee to Licensor in the quarterly statement following such examination.

Nondisclosure/Nonuse Agreement

1. The undersigned has been contacted by _____ (hereinafter the "Company") for the purpose of _____. The undersigned acknowledges that the Company has transmitted and will transmit certain concepts, designs, and ideas regarding its operation and craft products. The undersigned further acknowledges that the concepts, designs, ideas, and product information transmitted by the Company are considered proprietary information owned by the Company whether or not said information is protected under the copyright, patent, or trade secret laws of the United States or any state or country in the world.

2. In consideration for the Company revealing its proprietary information and continuing to deal with the undersigned, the undersigned agrees to receive the information transmitted by the Company in full confidence and that the information shall be reviewed and worked on in confidence. The undersigned shall not, without obtaining prior written consent of the Company, use, divulge, exploit, or in any way interfere with the rights of the Company in its proprietary information.

3. The undersigned further covenants that s/he/it shall not enter into competition with the Company, so long as such information remains confidential, anywhere in the United States or anywhere in the world, using the Company's designs, concepts, products, or ideas, or designs, concepts, products, or ideas substantially or confusingly similar to the Company's, or otherwise use the Company's designs, ideas, concepts, or products.

4. The undersigned acknowledges that money damages may be an inadequate remedy for resolving any dispute between the parties arising from this Agreement. The parties therefore agree that equitable remedies, such as injunction, are appropriate in enforcing this Agreement.

5. In the event that action, suit, or legal proceedings are initiated or brought to enforce any or all of the provisions of this Agreement, the prevailing party shall be entitled to such attorney fees, costs, and disbursements as are deemed reasonable and proper by an arbitrator or court. In the event of an appeal of an initial decision of an arbitrator or court, the prevailing party shall be entitled to such attorney fees, costs, and disbursements as are deemed reasonable and proper by the appellate court(s).

6. This Agreement shall be deemed executed in the State of [*State Where You Reside*] and shall be interpreted and construed in accordance with the laws of the State of [*State Where You Reside*] relating to contracts made and performed therein. Venue shall be proper only in the County of [*County Where You Reside*], State of [*State Where You Reside*].

Business Name

By: _____   _____

    Name: [Owner or Owner's Representative]   DATE

    Its: [Title]

Address: SSN or TID No.:

_____   _____

_____   _____

_____

Independent Contractor Agreement

BETWEEN: Name   ("Employer")
                       Address
                       Phone Number
                       Fax Number
                       E-mail Address

AND: Name   ("Independent"
                       Address   Contractor")
                       Phone Number
                       Fax Number
                       E-mail Address

Recitals

WHEREAS, Employer is engaged in the business of _____
_____; and

WHEREAS, Independent Contractor wishes to work for Employer, and Employer agrees to hire the Independent Contractor as _____
_____;

Agreement

NOW, THEREFORE, in consideration of the mutual covenants contained herein, the parties agree as follows:

1. Professional Performance. The Independent Contractor agrees to perform the work desired by Employer in a professional manner. It is expressly agreed by the Independent Contractor that the Independent Contractor's failure to properly complete any task requested by Employer shall be cause for termination of this Agreement.

2. Independent Contractor's Representations and Warranties. Independent Contractor represents and warrants that s/he will:

2.1   At her/his own expense, furnish all tools, materials, and equipment necessary to perform the services desired by Employer.

2.2   At her/his own expense, apply for and obtain all business registrations, permits, and licenses necessary to perform the services desired by Employer.

2.3   Be responsible for hiring, paying, supervising, and firing any employees necessary for proper completion of the services desired by Employer.

3. Work Made for Hire.

3.1   Ownership of Work Product. Independent Contractor agrees that the works s/he creates in the scope of her/his employment with Employer, and all intermediate works, including notes, outlines, and the like created in connection therewith (the "Work Product"), shall be the sole property of Employer upon fixation in a tangible medium of expression. Independent Contractor expressly acknowledges that the Work Product is to be considered a "work made for hire" within the meaning of the United States Copyright Act, as amended (the "Act"), and Employer is to be the "author" within the meaning of the Act. All copyrights in the Work Product, as well as all copies of such Work Product in any medium, shall be owned exclusively by Employer on their creation, and Independent Contractor expressly disclaims any interest in them.

3.2 **Assignment.** In the event (and to the extent) that the Work Product or any part of it is found as a matter of law not to be a work made for hire within the meaning of the Act, Independent Contractor hereby assigns to Employer the sole and exclusive right, title, and interest in and to the copyrights to, and all copies of, the Work Product without further consideration and agrees to assist Employer to register, and from time to time to enforce, the copyright. To that end, Independent Contractor agrees to execute and deliver all documents requested by Employer in connection therewith and irrevocably designates and appoints Employer as agent and attorney-in-fact to act for Independent Contractor and in her/his/its behalf and stead to execute, register, and file any such applications and to do other lawfully permitted acts to further the protection or registration of copyrights with the same legal force and effect as if executed by Independent Contractor.

3.3 **Other Intellectual Property.** Independent Contractor hereby assigns to Employer the sole and exclusive right, title, and interest in and to any intellectual property rights, including but not limited to patent, trademark and trade dress, and related goodwill, developed for Employer by Independent Contractor, without further consideration, and agrees to assist Employer to register, and from time to time to enforce, any such intellectual property. To that end, Independent Contractor agrees to execute and deliver all documents requested by Employer in connection therewith and irrevocably designates and appoints Employer as agent and attorney-in-fact to act for Independent Contractor and in its behalf and stead to execute, register, and file any such applications and to do other lawfully permitted acts to further the protection or registration of such intellectual property with the same legal force and effect as if executed by Independent Contractor.

3.4 **Independent Contractor's Intellectual Property.** In the event (and to the extent) that the Work Product contains any items or elements which may be proprietary to Independent Contractor or Independent Contractor's suppliers (if applicable), Independent Contractor hereby grants to Employer an irrevocable, perpetual, nonexclusive, royalty-free, worldwide license to reproduce, distribute copies of, prepare derivative works based on, display, and perform the Work Product and to authorize others to do any of the foregoing.

4. Confidentiality, Proprietary Information. The Independent Contractor may have access to trade secrets, customer lists, and other confidential information owned by Employer. In consideration for obtaining access to such information, the Independent Contractor hereby agrees that s/he shall be subject to the following restrictions:

4.1   The Independent Contractor acknowledges that information such as Employer's trade secrets, customer lists, and other confidential information is proprietary information, whether or not protected or protectable under copyright, patent, trademark, or any other law of the United States or any state. The Independent Contractor covenants that s/he will not use such information or divulge such information to any other person or use such information without the prior, express written permission of Employer.

4.2   Independent Contractor acknowledges Employer's exclusive right, title, and interest in and to Employer's intellectual property, and any registration that has issued or may issue thereon, and will not at any time do or cause to be done any act or thing contesting or in any way impairing or tending to impair part of such right, title, and interest. In connection with the use of such intellectual property, neither Independent Contractor nor any other party hereto shall in any manner represent that s/he has any ownership in the intellectual property or registrations thereof, and all parties acknowledge that use of such intellectual property shall enure to the benefit of Employer. Independent Contractor acknowledges that any intellectual property rights created by Independent Contractor during the term of this Agreement, including but not limited to copyrights, trademarks, trade dress, and patents, shall belong to Employer. Independent Contractor will execute and deliver to Employer such documents and take such other action as may be requested by Employer at any time and/or at the termination of this Agreement in order to assign, transfer, and convey any rights in and to such intellectual property that Independent Contractor may acquire.

4.3   The Independent Contractor also covenants that s/he will not, during the term of this Agreement and for a period of three (3) years after termination of this Agreement, compete, directly or indirectly, with Employer in the State of [*State Where You Reside*] or in any other state in which Employer is doing business, in the field of _____ .

4.4   Because of the unique nature of Employer's business, the Independent Contractor agrees that this restriction is reasonable. In the event that a court or arbitrator finds that such a restriction is unreasonable, the parties agree that the court or arbitrator may establish geographical and temporal limits that are reasonable in scope. In addition to and independent of the provision of Paragraph 2.3, in order to ensure with compliance with the terms of this Agreement, and in order to allow Employer to evaluate risks to its proprietary and confidential information, the Independent Contractor agrees to notify Employer prior to accepting any employment or appointment as an employee, independent contractor, consultant, officer, or director, or investing in or commencing any business related to Employer's business.

4.5   Independent Contractor agrees that, upon termination of the independent contractor relationship with Employer, Independent Contractor will return to Employer all of Employer's property in her/his possession or control, including but not limited to any papers, books, and disks containing Employer's trade secrets and other confidential information. Independent Contractor further represents that s/he will purge from all computers used by her/him (other than those on Employer's premises) all files pertaining to Employer or containing Employer's information, and that s/he will retain no backup disks, tapes, or other storage devices containing such information.

4.6 The terms of this Section 2 shall survive termination of this Agreement for any reason.

5. Compensation. In consideration for the foregoing, Employer agrees to pay the Independent Contractor at the rate of _____ dollars ($_____) per _____.

6. Term. The term of this Agreement shall be __ (__) year, unless extended by Employer within _____ (__) days prior to the date of termination.

7. Independent Contractor. The relationship of Employer and Independent Contractor shall be that of an independent contractor. Employer shall not be responsible for income tax, Social Security, Workers' Compensation, unemployment insurance, or any other withholding or payment as an employer, nor shall Employer be responsible for any acts or omissions of Independent Contractor or Independent Contractor's agents. Independent Contractor agrees to hold Employer harmless from and against any and all liability (including reasonable attorneys' fees incurred on trial or appeal) resulting from or in any way connected to Independent Contractor's or his/her agent's negligent acts or omissions.

8. Assignability. This Agreement or the rights, responsibilities, or obligations granted or assumed in this Agreement may not be assigned by either party hereunder, in whole or in part, except to a corporation in which a party is the majority shareholder, without first obtaining the written consent of both parties hereto. If Independent Contractor consents to assignment of this Agreement by Employer, then such assignment will include but not be limited to all provisions related to intellectual property and noncompetition, to any purchaser of a majority of all significant assets of Employer or to any division of Employer. This Agreement shall be binding upon and inure to the benefit of the parties and their respective heirs and legal representatives.

9. Notices. All notices required by this Agreement shall be made in writing, postage prepaid, certified mail, return receipt requested, or by facsimile transmission to the addresses or numbers first given above, or by hand delivery. Notice shall be deemed received two (2) days after the date of mailing or the day after it is faxed, e-mailed, or hand delivered.

10. Attorney Fees. Whether or not an action, suit, or legal proceedings is initiated or brought to enforce any or all of the provisions of this Agreement, the prevailing party shall be entitled to such attorney fees, costs, and disbursements as are deemed reasonable and proper by an arbitrator or court. In the event of an appeal of an initial decision of an arbitrator or court, the prevailing party shall be entitled to such attorney fees, costs, and disbursements as are deemed reasonable and proper by the appellate court(s).

11. Venue. This Agreement shall be deemed executed in the State of [*State Where You Reside*] and shall be interpreted and construed in accordance with the laws of the State of [*State Where You Reside*] relating to contracts made and performed therein. Venue shall be proper only in the County of [*County Where You Reside*], State of [*State Where You Reside*].

12. Merger. This Agreement constitutes the entire agreement between the parties and supersedes all prior agreements, understandings, and proposals (whether written or oral) in respect to the matters specified.

13. Modification. No alteration, modification, amendment, addition, deletion, or change to this Agreement shall be effective or binding unless and until such alterations, modifications, amendments, additions, deletions, or changes are properly executed in writing by both parties.

14. Headings. All headings used in this Agreement are for reference purposes only and are not intended or deemed to limit or affect, in any way, the meaning or interpretation of any of the terms and provisions of this Agreement.

15. Rule of Construction. It is expressly agreed by the parties to this Agreement that the rule of construction that a document should be more strictly interpreted against the person who drafted it shall not apply to any provision.

16. Waiver. No waiver by either party of any breach or default hereunder shall be deemed a waiver of any repetition of such breach or default or in any way affect any of the other terms and conditions hereof.

17. Severability. If any provision of this Agreement is judicially declared to be invalid, unenforceable, or void by a court of competent jurisdiction, such decision shall not have the effect of invalidating or voiding the remainder of this Agreement, and the part(s) of this Agreement so held to be invalid, unenforceable or void shall be deemed stricken, and the Agreement will be reformed to replace such stricken provision with a valid and enforceable provision which comes as close as possible to expressing the intention of the stricken provision. The remainder of this Agreement shall have the same force and effect as if such part or parts had never been included.

18. Effective Date. This Agreement is effective as of the date all parties hereto have executed this Agreement.

19. Counterparts. This Agreement may be executed in two (2) or more counterparts, each of which shall be deemed an original, but all of which together shall constitute one and the same Agreement.

EMPLOYER
[Business Name]

By: _____   _____
    Name: [You or Your Representative]   DATE
    Its: [Title]

INDEPENDENT CONTRACTOR

_____   _____
Name: [Independent Contractor's Name]   DATE
SSN: _____

Employment Agreement

BETWEEN: Name   ("Employer")
                             Address
                             Phone Number
                             Fax Number
                             E-mail Address

AND: Name   ("Employee")
                             Address
                             Phone Number
                             Fax Number
                             E-mail Address

Recitals

WHEREAS, Employer is engaged in the business of _____; and

WHEREAS, Employee wishes to work for Employer, and Employer agrees to employ the Employee;

Agreement

NOW, THEREFORE, in consideration of the mutual covenants contained herein, the parties agree as follows:

1. Professional Performance. The Employee agrees to perform the work desired by Employer in a professional manner. It is expressly agreed by the Employee that the Employee's failure to complete any task as directed by Employer shall be cause for termination of this Agreement. Employee represents that s/he has examined the workplace and is fully informed regarding all hazards of the job, including but not limited to uses and identity of hazardous substances.

2. Confidentiality and Covenant Not to Compete. The Employee may have access to trade secrets, customer lists, sales materials, and other confidential information owned by Employer. In consideration for obtaining access to such information, the Employee hereby agrees that s/he shall be subject to the following restrictions:

    2.1   The Employee shall, at all times, provide services to Employer under Employer's control and direction.

    2.2   The Employee acknowledges that information such as Employer's trade secrets, customer lists, sales materials and information, and other confidential information is proprietary information, whether or not protected or protectable under copyright, patent, trademark, or any other law of the United States or any state. The Employee covenants that s/he will not use such information or divulge such information to any other person without the prior, express written permission of Employer.

    2.3   The Employee also covenants that s/he will not, during the period of employment with Employer and for a period of three (3) years after termination of employment compete, directly or indirectly, with Employer in the State of [*State Where You Reside*] or in any other state in which Employer does business.

2.4 Because of the unique nature of Employer's business, the Employee agrees that this restriction is reasonable. In the event that a court or arbitrator finds that such a restriction is unreasonable, the parties agree that the court or arbitrator may establish geographical and temporal limits that are reasonable in scope. In addition to and independent of the provision of Paragraph 2.3, in order to ensure with compliance with the terms of this Agreement, and in order to allow Employer to evaluate risks to its proprietary and confidential information, the Employee agrees to notify Employer prior to accepting any employment or appointment as an employee, independent contractor, consultant, officer, or director, or investing in or commencing any business related to Employer's business.

2.5 Employee agrees that, at the termination of her/his employment, Employee will return to Employer all of Employer's property in her/his possession or control, including but not limited to any papers, books, and disks containing Employer's trade secrets and other confidential information. Employee further represents that s/he will purge from all computers used by her/him (other than those on Employer's premises) all files pertaining to Employer or containing Employer's information, and that s/he will retain no backup disks, tapes, or other storage devices containing such information.

2.6 The terms of this Section 2 shall survive termination of this Agreement for any reason.

3. Intellectual Property. Employee acknowledges Employer's exclusive right, title, and interest in and to Employer's intellectual property, and any registration that has issued or may issue thereon, and will not at any time do or cause to be done any act or thing contesting or in any way impairing or tending to impair part of such right, title, and interest. In connection with the use of such intellectual property, neither Employee nor any other party hereto shall in any manner represent that s/he has any ownership in the intellectual property or registrations thereof, and all parties acknowledge that use of such intellectual property shall enure to the benefit of Employer. Employee acknowledges that any intellectual property rights created by Employee during the term of this Agreement, including but not limited to copyrights, trademarks, trade dress, and patents, shall belong to Employer. Employee will execute and deliver to Employer such documents and take such other action as may be requested by Employer at any time and/or at the termination of this Agreement in order to assign, transfer, and convey to Employer any rights in and to such intellectual property that Employee may acquire.

4. Compensation. In consideration for the foregoing, Employer agrees to pay the Employee at the rate of _____ dollars ($_____) per _____ .

5. Policies. Employee agrees to abide by and comply with all of Employer's policies currently in effect and as later modified.

6. At Will Employment. This contract may be revoked, terminated, or modified at any time by Employer in its sole discretion, with or without cause, without notice and without any liability on the part of Employer.

7. Mandatory Arbitration. Any controversy arising out of or relating to this Agreement, or breach thereof, shall be resolved by binding arbitration conducted by the American Arbitration Association. Such arbitration shall be held in [*County Where Your Business Is Located*] County, [*State Where Your Business Is Located*], and shall be in accordance with the applicable Commercial Arbitration Rules of the American Arbitration Association which are in effect at the time the demand for arbitration is made. Any award rendered by the arbitrator(s) may be entered in any court having jurisdiction thereof and may include reasonable attorney fees and costs to the prevailing party. In any such arbitration, the parties shall have all of the rights and methods of discovery as provided for by the applicable Rules of Civil Procedure for the [*State Where Your Business Is Located*], as if the subject matter of the arbitration were pending in a civil action before a Circuit Court in the State of [*State Where Your Business Is Located*]. Any discovery disputes shall also be decided by the arbitrator appointed to hear the main arbitration.

8. Assignability. This Agreement or the rights, responsibilities, or obligations granted or assumed in this Agreement may not be assigned by either party hereunder, in whole or in part, without first obtaining the written consent of both parties hereto. If Employee consents to assignment of this Agreement by Employer, then such assignment will include but not be limited to all provisions related to intellectual property and noncompetition, to any purchaser of a majority of all significant assets of Employer or to any division of Employer.

9. Notices. All notices required by this Agreement shall be made in writing, postage prepaid, certified mail, return receipt requested, or by facsimile transmission to the addresses or numbers first given above, or by hand delivery. Notice shall be deemed received two (2) days after the date of mailing or the day after it is faxed or hand delivered.

10. Attorney Fees. Whether or not an action, suit, or legal proceeding is initiated or brought to enforce any or all of the provisions of this Agreement, the prevailing party shall be entitled to such attorney fees, costs, and disbursements as are deemed reasonable and proper by an arbitrator or court. In the event of an appeal of an initial decision of an arbitrator or court, the prevailing party shall be entitled to such attorney fees, costs, and disbursements as are deemed reasonable and proper by the appellate court(s).

11. Venue. This Agreement shall be deemed executed in the State of [*State Where You Reside*] and shall be interpreted and construed in accordance with the laws of the State of [*State Where You Reside*] relating to contracts made and performed therein. Venue shall be proper only in the County of [*County Where You Reside*], State of [*State Where You Reside*].

12. Merger. This Agreement constitutes the entire agreement between the parties and supersedes all prior agreements, understandings, and proposals (whether written or oral) in respect to the matters specified.

13. Modification. No alteration, modification, amendment, addition, deletion, or change to this Agreement shall be effective or binding unless and until such alterations, modifications, amendments, additions, deletions, or changes are properly executed in writing by both parties.

14. Headings. All headings used in this Agreement are for reference purposes only and are not intended or deemed to limit or affect, in any way, the meaning or interpretation of any of the terms and provisions of this Agreement.

15. Rule of Construction. It is expressly agreed by the parties to this Agreement that the rule of construction that a document should be more strictly interpreted against the person who drafted it shall not apply to any provision.

16. Waiver. No waiver by either party of any breach or default hereunder shall be deemed a waiver of any repetition of such breach or default or in any way affect any of the other terms and conditions hereof.

17. Severability. If any provision of this Agreement is judicially declared to be invalid, unenforceable, or void by a court of competent jurisdiction, such decision shall not have the effect of invalidating or voiding the remainder of this Agreement, and the part(s) of this Agreement so held to be invalid, unenforceable or void shall be deemed stricken, and the Agreement will be reformed to replace such stricken provision with a valid and enforceable provision which comes as close as possible to expressing the intention of the stricken provision. The remainder of this Agreement shall have the same force and effect as if such part or parts had never been included.

18. Effective Date. This Agreement is effective as of the date all parties hereto have executed this Agreement.

19. Counterparts. This Agreement may be executed in two (2) or more counterparts, each of which shall be deemed an original, but all of which together shall constitute one and the same Agreement.

EMPLOYER
[Business Name]

By: _____   _____

     Name: [You or Your Representative]   DATE
     Its: [Title]

EMPLOYEE

_____   _____

Name: [Employee's Name]   DATE
SSN: _____

Employment At Will and Arbitration Agreement

1. It is agreed by and between _____ ("Employee") and _____ ("Employer") that the Employer or Employee can terminate the employment and compensation of Employee at any time, with or without cause and/or with or without advance notice, at the option of Employer or Employee.

2. It is further agreed that Employee and Employer will utilize binding arbitration to resolve all disputes that may arise out of the employment context. Both Employer and Employee agree that any claim, dispute and/or controversy that either Employee may have against Employee (or its owners, directors, officers, managers, employees, agents and parties affiliated with its employee benefit and health plans) or Employer may have against Employee arising from, related to or having any relationship or connection whatsoever with Employee seeking employment with, employment by or other association with Employer shall be submitted to and determined exclusively by binding arbitration under the Federal Arbitration Act in conformity with the procedures of the [*State Where You Reside*] Employment Act.

Included within the scope of this Agreement are all disputes, whether based on tort, contract, statute (including but not limited to any claims of discrimination or harassment, whether they be based on the [*State Where Your Business Is Located*]'s fair employment practices laws, Title VII of the Civil Rights Act of 1964, as amended, or any other state, local or federal laws or regulations), equitable law or otherwise, with the exception of claims arising under the National Labor Relations Act which are brought before the National Labor Relations Board, claims for medical and disability benefits under state workers' compensation laws, administrative claims for unemployment benefits or as otherwise required by law. Nothing herein, however, shall prevent Employee from filing and pursuing administrative remedies (although, if Employee chooses to pursue a claim following the exhaustion of such administrative remedies, that claim would be subject to the provisions of this Agreement).

In addition to requirements imposed by law, any arbitrator herein shall be a retired [*State Where Your Business is Located*] Circuit Court judge (or other similarly qualified individual with arbitration experience as mutually agreed to by the parties) and shall be subject to disqualification on the same grounds as would apply to a judge of such court. To the extent applicable in civil actions in U.S. District Court, the following shall apply and be observed: all rules of pleading, all rules of evidence, all rights to discovery and all rights to resolution of the dispute by means of motions for summary judgment and judgment on the pleadings. Resolution of the dispute shall be based solely upon the law governing the claims and defenses set forth in the pleadings, and the arbitrator may not invoke any basis (including but not limited to notions of "just cause") other than such controlling law. The arbitrator shall have the immunity of a judicial officer from civil liability when acting in the capacity of an arbitrator, which immunity supplements any other existing immunity. Likewise, all communications during or in connection with the arbitration proceedings are privileged. As reasonably required to allow full use and benefit of this Agreement, the arbitrator shall extend the times for the giving of notices and setting of hearings. Awards shall include the arbitrator's written reasoned opinion.

If any provision of this Agreement is judicially declared to be invalid, unenforceable or void by a court of competent jurisdiction, such decision shall not have the effect of invalidating or voiding the remainder of this Agreement, and the part(s) of this Agreement so held to be invalid, unenforceable or void shall be deemed stricken, and the Agreement will be reformed to replace such stricken provision with a valid and enforceable provision which comes as close as possible to expressing the intention of the stricken provision. The remainder of this Agreement shall have the same force and effect as if such part or parts had never been included.

EMPLOYEE UNDERSTANDS AND AGREES TO THIS BINDING ARBITRA-TION PROVISION, AND BOTH EMPLOYEE AND EMPLOYER GIVE UP THEIR RIGHT TO TRIAL BY JURY OF ANY CLAIM EMPLOYEE OR EMPLOYER MAY HAVE AGAINST THE OTHER.

3. This is the entire agreement between Employer and Employee regarding dispute resolution, the length of any employment and the reasons for termination of employment, and this Agreement supersedes any and all prior agreements regarding these issues.

4. It is further agreed and understood that any agreement contrary to the terms of this Agreement must be entered into, in writing, by the President of Employer. No supervisor representative of Employer other than its President has any authority to enter into any agreement for employment for any specified period of time or make any agreement contrary to the terms of this Agreement. *Oral representations made before or after Employee is hired do not alter this Agreement.*

MY SIGNATURE BELOW ATTESTS TO THE FACT THAT I HAVE READ, UNDERSTAND, AND AGREE TO BE LEGALLY BOUND TO ALL OF THE ABOVE TERMS.

Signed at _____, [*State Where You Reside*] this _____ day of _____, 2____.

Employee's signature _____

INITIALS OF APPLICANT _____

INITIALS OF EMPLOYER REPRESENTATIVE _____

At Will Employment Form

It has become common for employers to require new employees to sign a statement acknowledging that the employment is at will and does not give rise to any contractual right. Such a statement might read:

Dear Employer:

I have just been hired to work as a _____.[1]
I understand that my employment is at will and that I can be terminated or I may quit at any time without any prior notice. You have made no representation to me regarding the position other than the salary, working period, holiday schedule, and general description of the work to be performed, and I am relying on no other representations except those which are embodied in or attached to this letter.[2]

I shall work diligently for you and use my best effort to honestly complete the tasks you have assigned to me.

_____

(New Employee)

---

[1]Describe in some detail the job to be performed.
[2]If there are any specific statements, such as a right to purchase the finished product at a discount or the right to have a paid vacation, these should be specified, attached to this letter, and the sheet upon which they appear should be initialed by employer and the new employee, or such information might be discussed in the Employee Handbook.

APPENDIX D: USEFUL FORMS

Recording Business Deductions

	Travel	Entertainment	Gifts
Amount of Money	Make separate categories for transportation, food, lodging, etc.[1]	This needs separate categories for food, entertainment, taxis, etc.[2]	Cost.[3]
Time and Date	Beginning and ending dates. (Be sure to separate business days from pleasure days.)	Date. If entertainment occurred directly before or after a business discussion, note the time spent discussing business.	Date.
Place	City or destination.	Name, address, type of entertainment, if not apparent from the name of the place where business discussion was held. Note whether entertainment was before, during, or after the discussion.	N/A
Description	N/A	N/A	Description of gift.
Business Purpose	Business reason for travel, what business benefit you expected to gain.	Business reason, what business benefit you expect to gain, nature of business discussed.	Business reason for making gift; what business benefit you expected to gain.
Business Relationship	N/A	Names, occupations, titles of people entertained, showing their business relationship to you; list only those people who engaged in the business discussion.[4]	Names, occupations, titles of recipients, showing their business relationship to you.

(See next page for footnote references)

---

[1]You can total the daily cost of your meals and other incidentals (i.e., gas, oil, phone calls, taxis, cleaning, tips), so long as they are listed in reasonable categories.

[2]Incidental costs can be totaled daily.

[3]You may not deduct gifts worth more than $25 per person.

[4]If you entertain a large group of people, you do not need to list their names separately if they belong to a readily identifiable group. You may not deduct club fees unless you can prove that more than 50 percent of the use of the club is for business purposes. Each separate payment (i.e., dinner and theater) is usually considered a separate expense and should be recorded as such. Documentary evidence in the form of a receipt is necessary to support all lodging expenses and any other expense more than $75, except for transportation expenses like taxis. Documentary evidence is generally sufficient if it shows the amount, date, place, and essential character of the expense. For example, a hotel receipt is sufficient if it includes the name, address, dates, and separate charges for meals and telephone.

Letter Requesting Permission to Use Copyrighted Material

Dear [*Copyright Owner*]:[1]

    I am in the process of dealing with _____.[2] In the course of my research, I discovered your excellent piece[3] and would like permission to reproduce it.[4]

    Enclosed for your convenience is a release form and a stamped, self-addressed envelope.

    Thank you very much for your cooperation.

Sincerely,

_____

RELEASE

I hereby grant [*Your Name*] the right to reproduce my copyrighted work in connection with _____.[2] I understand that [*Your Name*] will acknowledge me as the creator of _____[3] and include my copyright notice on the work when it is reproduced.

_____
                   (Signature)

---

[1]This letter should be addressed to the name appearing in the copyright notice. If you have difficulty locating the copyright owner's address and if the work is registered, you can obtain it from the Copyright Office.

[2]Describe in detail the purpose for which you are requesting permission to reproduce the work. Some pursuits, such as teaching or academic writing, are customarily not charged for reproduction rights, whereas others, such as commercial exploitation, are. If there is any possibility that a charge may be imposed, you may want to add a sentence such as, "If there is any charge for the reproduction right, please advise me as soon as possible."

[3]Identify as specifically as possible the work you wish to reproduce, as well as the location of the work. For example, if you wish to reproduce a design that appears in a book on textiles, state the title of the book, the date published, and the page on which the design appears.

[4]You should specify with some clarity the purpose for which the permission is being granted, i.e., to reproduce, to display, to sell, to modify, to perform, etc.

APPENDIX E:
COLLECTING YOUR DEBTS

Collecting past due accounts can be difficult. Despite all precautions, it is inevitable that you will wind up with some overdue accounts. The following is an example of a letter written to collect an outstanding bill. You may wish to use it as a model for your own debt collection letters.

COLLECTION LETTER SAMPLE

CERTIFIED MAIL NO. _____
RETURN RECEIPT REQUESTED

Re: Invoice No. _____

Dear _____:
On January 3, 2005, you purchased a stained glass window from me for $500. You paid $200 down and agreed to pay the balance within 60 days after receiving the window. A good deal of time has elapsed since the window was delivered to you, and I have not received the promised payment.

I, therefore, make demand upon you for $300 within 10 days from the date of this letter, or I will have no alternative other than to institute litigation against you. In the event that litigation is commenced, you may be held liable not only for the amount due but also for court costs [and attorney fees].[1]

Please be advised that federal law gives you 30 days after you receive this letter to dispute the validity of the debt or any part of it. If you do not dispute it within that period, I will assume that it is valid. If you do dispute it, by notifying me in writing to that effect, I will, as required by the law, mail to you proof of the debt.[2]

The law does not require me to wait until the end of the 30-day period before suing you to collect this debt. If, however, you request proof of the debt or the name and address of the original creditor within the 30-day period that begins with your receipt of this letter, the law requires me to then suspend my efforts (through litigation or otherwise) to collect the debt until I mail the requested information to you. This letter is an attempt to collect a debt, and any information obtained will be used only for that purpose.

Sincerely,

_____

---

[1] Do not allege liability for attorney fees unless you have concluded that you have a right to recover them. If your contract provided for attorney fees in case of litigation to enforce the contract, they should be recoverable. If you did not have a contract or there was not an attorney fees clause, you will have to determine whether your state permits the recovery of attorney fees in lawsuits for debt collection. A lawyer should be able to answer this question for you.

[2] If you are not the original creditor, then substitute the following language for the last sentence of this paragraph:

> If you do dispute it, by notifying me in writing to that effect, I will, as required by the law, obtain and mail to you proof of the debt. If, within the same period, you request in writing the name and address of your original creditor, if the creditor is different from the current creditor, I will furnish you with that information.

INDEX

Books from Allworth Press

Allworth Press is an imprint of Allworth Communications, Inc. Selected titles are listed below.

Business and Legal Forms for Crafts, Second Edition
by Tad Crawford (paperback, includes CD-ROM, 8⅜ × 10⅞, 144 pages, $29.95)

Licensing Art & Design, Revised Edition
by Caryn R. Leland (paperback, 6 × 9, 128 pages, $16.95)

Legal Guide for the Visual Artist, Fourth Edition
by Tad Crawford (paperback, 8½ × 11, 272 pages, $19.95)

Selling Your Crafts, Revised Edition
by Susan Joy Sager (paperback, 6 × 9, $19.95, 288 pages)

Creating a Successful Crafts Business
by Rogene A. Robbins and Robert Robbins (paperback, 6 × 9, 256 pages, $19.95)

The Business of Being an Artist, Third Edition
by Daniel Grant (paperback, 6 × 9, 352 pages, $19.95)

Crafts and Craft Shows: How to Make Money
by Philip Kadubec (paperback, 6 × 9, 208 pages, $16.95)

The Artist's Complete Health and Safety Guide, Third Edition
by Monona Rossol (paperback, 6 × 9, 416 pages, $19.95)

The Fine Artist's Guide to Marketing and Self-Promotion, Revised Edition
by Julius Vitali (paperback, 6 × 9, 256 pages, $19.95)

Make Money Quilting
by Sylvia Ann Landman (paperback, 6 × 9, 256 pages, $19.95)

Creative Careers in Crafts
by Susan Joy Sager (paperback, 6 × 9, 272 pages, $19.95)